What Your Colleagues Are Saying . . .

MW00565383

"This book is the answer to one of the most vexing problems teachers—how to handle those endless (and dreaded) stacks of pape the answers provided help teachers and even more importantly, help *students*.

"I wish I had this book years ago—it would have saved me from the dread of facing stacks of essays as well as the hours spent 'grading' those essays in ways that didn't really help students. I wish every student could receive this kind of 'flash' feedback—it stands to move writers in significant and life-changing ways, without burning out their teachers in the process."

—Berit Gordon, author
No More Fake Reading: Merging the Classics
With Independent Reading to Create Joyful, Lifelong Readers

"Looking for trusty ways to make writing feedback efficient and effective? Aren't we all! Lucky for us, Matthew Johnson shares them here. I know that what he shares here is worth its salt because he has vetted it himself—in his classroom and while staring down a stack of papers. What I love most about this book is that it speaks to the heart of every writing teacher's purpose and mission. Equally, Matt shares practical feedback moves that writing teachers must have to be the best for their students and themselves."

—Patty McGee, author
Feedback That Moves Writers Forward:
How to Escape Correcting Mode to Transform Student Writing

"'Grading student writing is so demoralizing,' said no teacher who ever read *Flash Feedback*. The actionable tips and resources in this book help teachers arrange writing instruction for their students so that feedback is placed where it will have the greatest impact while simultaneously redeeming all those hours lost shuttling stacks of papers to and from school. Matthew M. Johnson puts writing teachers on a path that leads away from teacher-guilt toward a life of balance."

—Jeffery E. Frieden, author
Make Them Process It: Uncovering
New Value in the Writer's Notebook

"Matthew Johnson's book *Flash Feedback* will be received with cheers by teachers of all content areas. . . . His approach finally gives teachers permission to prioritize student needs without sacrificing work-life balance. He synthesizes and simplifies research-based practices that will increase our effectiveness as teachers of writing while maintaining a manageable workload.

"I recommend this book to any teacher who wants to improve his or her students' writing but who, like me, feels buried in the constant cycle of grading."

—Meagan Wright, 7th grade language arts teacher
Alston Ridge Middle School, Cary, NC

"Matthew Johnson hits the proverbial nail on the head with *Flash Feedback*, solving what English teachers have struggled with for years: spending far too much time grading written work in 'autopsy' mode, rather than providing authentic, quick, and meaningful feedback to students. Based on sound research and evidence, Johnson validates the frustration that those of us who teach writing experience every day and offers a step-by-step guide to what should be the new best practices for student writing achievement. Whether you are a veteran or novice English teacher, *Flash Feedback* should be your new 'go to' manual for truly improving student writing—and saving your own teacher sanity in the process."

—David Krzisnik, English Language Arts Instructor
Salem High School, *Plymouth-Canton* Community Schools

"Johnson blends research-based feedback protocols with students *and* teachers in mind. Within these pages, readers encounter strategies that encourage students to develop their own writing goals, reflect upon and respond to feedback as writers, and enter into a process of writing that creates confidence. In *Flash Feedback*, teachers learn how to accomplish all of this *and still* save time for themselves. With his latest work, Johnson has given teachers the gift of time without sacrificing substance."

—Andrew Schoenborn, co-author
Creating Confident Writers

Flash Feedback

Once again to Cat

Flash Feedback

Responding to Student Writing Better and Faster—Without Burning Out

Matthew Johnson

Foreword by Dave Stuart Jr.

CORWIN Literacy

FOR INFORMATION:

Corwin

A SAGE Company

2455 Teller Road

Thousand Oaks, California 91320

(800) 233-9936

www.corwin.com

SAGE Publications Ltd.

1 Oliver's Yard

55 City Road

London EC1Y 1SP

United Kingdom

SAGE Publications India Pvt. Ltd.

B 1/I 1 Mohan Cooperative Industrial Area

Mathura Road, New Delhi 110 044

India

SAGE Publications Asia-Pacific Pte. Ltd.

18 Cross Street #10-10/11/12

China Square Central

Singapore 048423

Acquisitions Editor: Tori Bachman

Editorial Development Manager: Julie Nemer

Senior Editorial Assistant: Sharon Wu

Production Editor: Amy Schroller

Copy Editor: Deanna Noga

Typesetter: C&M Digitals (P) Ltd.

Proofreader: Lawrence W. Baker

Indexer: Wendy Allex

Cover Designer: Rose Storey

Marketing Manager: Deena Meyer

Printed in Canada

ISBN 978-1-5443-6049-2

This book is printed on acid-free paper.

20 21 22 23 24 10 9 8 7 6 5 4 3 2 1

Contents

Visit the companion website at
resources.corwin.com/flashfeedback
for related links and downloadable resources.

Foreword

Here's a statement that doesn't need stating: teaching is good, important, *pressure-filled* work.

All the teachers I know got into the work because they wanted to promote the long-term flourishing of young people by way of helping them master the disciplines. Writing teachers like you and me are no different—when we were new, we hoped that, through helping our students master the written word, we'd unleash their potential and open up a whole new means for accessing the power of their hearts and minds. We aimed at nothing less than emancipation—after all, writing had had this kind of effect on us.

And boy oh boy, were we *wise* to endeavor toward that. Our hearts were noble and beautiful because teaching is good and important work.

But then we got into our first teaching gigs, and we taught our students to write those first essays or stories or poems, and all of a sudden a new character entered our personal stories: a stack of papers. Our students had poured themselves into these things. And we thought, "Oh. Well, I guess it's time to give feedback on these."

This was fine at first! After all, we had signed up for this. The only problem was that this feedback took so much *time*. Before we knew it, that stack of papers followed us everywhere. It developed its own little indent in our teacher bags. And it had this weird and disturbing tendency toward *growing*. No matter how many papers we feedbacked, this thing just seemed to keep getting bigger.

And we heard, for the first time, that question we had once asked some of our own writing teachers. "Hey, Mr. Stuart: Have you had a chance to read our papers yet?"

Oh no, we realized. That stack of papers isn't just any character in our lives.

It's a monster.

What on earth had we gotten ourselves into?

As Matt Johnson quickly points out in the pages that follow, the indomitable feedback monster is an old beast for writing teachers. I love that Matt finds, in the earliest edition of the *English Journal*, an article lamenting the weight of the writing teacher's paper load. This was in 1912. Talk about confirmation that today's pressing problems are often the pressing problems of our predecessors. Over a century later, it looks like Solomon was right: there's nothing new under the sun.

When I first met Matt, we were at a pub in Cedar Springs, Michigan, eating lunch and enjoying authentic German microbrews. Matt had emailed me months before, asking if he might drive across the state to discuss some questions he had about the teacher–writer life. Lunch was on him, he said—and so, I delightedly agreed. By the time the tab arrived, I had given Matt a daunting list of recommendations regarding how I would start a blog for teachers if I were starting one today, what my long-term vision for that blog might be, and what the publishing landscape was like in teacher books, from my perspective.

Within a year, Matt's blog was being read by thousands of readers each month, his work was being featured on Edutopia, and he was in talks with Corwin Literacy for a book contract. That book is the one you now hold in your hand.

Matt Johnson is *that* good, I thought. But now, having read this book, I see it differently: his sense of urgency is that strong.

So here's the good news for every teacher I know: teaching *is* an incredible way to promote the long-term flourishing of lots of young people. I can't think of a better way, actually. It is beautiful and important and reverberating work, even in 2020 as Matt's book is being published.

And for us teachers of writing: we weren't crazy. Teaching our students to write well *does* unleash their potential, and it *does* open up a whole new means for accessing the power of their hearts and minds. Writing *is* that important. It *is* emancipatory.

And as Matt shares in these pages, there's a way to do this work that doesn't require us to make peace with the paper monster. There's a way to *do* feedback well, and to do it efficiently, and to do it humanely.

For Matt Johnson—and for all of us now, thanks to Matt's book—flash feedback isn't just a theory. It's a reality.

Best to you, my colleague, as you enjoy and apply Matt's book. I'll be doing the same for years to come!

Dave Stuart Jr.
Cedar Springs, MI

Acknowledgments

As I look at this book, I can't help but feel that dozens, if not hundreds, of names should be written on the cover alongside mine. This is because everything inside that cover comes from the numerous ghostwriters who have inspired, informed, critiqued, and cultivated my teaching and writing over the last 15 years.

While I am supposedly a writer, I know that my words will fail me when it comes to properly thanking them all for everything they've given to me. Even still, I would like to give it a shot.

First, thank you to all my students. While I am technically your teacher, no better teacher exists than you all. You uplift, challenge, affirm, and change me for the better every day.

Thank you as well to the best English department anywhere: Ken, Judith, Tracy, and Robert. I am amazed and informed by the teaching magic that floats out of your rooms on a daily basis.

To other incredible writing teachers I've worked with—David, Kelly, Gretchen, Aletia, Meghan, Amy, Jenna, Heidi, Gail, Eachan, Emily, Celinda, and many others—getting to learn from and observe you is why I am the teacher I am today.

Also, I want to give a sincere thanks to all those administrators who have supported my growth as a teacher, especially Marci, Rebecca, Karen, Ann, Gary, Peter, Carmie, and Debbie.

Big bear hugs to the three editors who've taken a chance on me: Tom Koerner, Lisa Luedeke, and especially Tori Bachman, who crafted this book alongside me.

I also want to acknowledge all those brilliant educators who graciously shared their ideas with the world so that I could borrow and build on them here. A particular thanks to Kelly Gallagher, Tom Newkirk, Alison Marchetti, Rebekah O'Dell, Nancy Frey and Douglas Fisher, Carol Jago, Linda Rief, Nancy Steinke, Patty McGee, Barry Gilmore, Jeff Anderson, and Jim Burke.

To Linda Christensen, who opened her classroom and her heart up to me; Dave Stuart Jr., who spent an entire afternoon helping a teacher from downstate whom he didn't even know find his voice; and Ken McGraw, who was the best mentor and friend any young teacher could dream of—I know this book wouldn't exist without you.

Thank you as well to my family and friends for the support you gave me through the twists and turns of writing a book, my dad for teaching me to love words, my mom for showing me how to teach from my heart, my brother for always being there for me, and the whole McGarry clan.

To my children Maya and Wesley, it is no coincidence that I embarked on this book after you entered my life. I am inspired by you every day.

The biggest of all thank-yous to the best partner, friend, muse, and editor I have ever known—Cat, I am thankful every hour of every day that I turned right instead of left when leaving my house that day nearly 15 years ago. This book is for and because of you most of all.

Thank you as well to all my readers. Your time is your most valuable asset, and I am so thankful that you entrusted some with me.

And finally, to every teacher out there building, supporting, inspiring, and culti-vating his or her students. Your work happens quietly and often without fanfare, but never forget that you change the world every single day. This book is for you.

Publisher's Acknowledgments

Barry Gilmore
Principal
Hutchison School
Memphis, TN

Jennifer Wheat Townsend
Director of Learning
Noblesville Schools
Noblesville, IN

Andy Schoenborn
ELA and Literacy Teacher
Mount Pleasant High School
Mount Pleasant, MI

Introduction

There's an afternoon about a decade ago that stands out in my mind. I sat at my desk and stared at the stacks of paper amassing on it. There must have been at least six inches of slightly crumpled student essays clasped together with oversized clips, all waiting for response. I thought through the familiar checklist for how I would handle the load: Brew some extra coffee and grade late into the night most evenings for the next couple weeks. Sneak some essays into the stands to grade during my wife's hockey game. Grade a few more in the waiting room as my car gets an oil change. Trade lunch breaks for wolfing down a soup or sandwich with one hand while the other works through a couple more papers. Probably burn a personal day plodding through the rest at a coffee shop before the quarter grades are due.

Sound familiar?

I was in my third year of teaching. This wasn't my first time staring down a stack of writing that size, but for some reason this pile of papers came with a sudden realization: I couldn't live like this much longer. While I deeply loved being a teacher, the seemingly never-ending papers in need of comments and grades acted as a great many straws about to break this camel's back. I was already overloaded with planning, teaching, meetings, data collection, email, and the myriad other tasks that a teacher must do. I knew I couldn't sustain this paper load and continue to be an effective teacher, let alone a decent partner, friend, parent, and human.

If I couldn't find a way to spend less time with papers to make room for spending more time on family, friends, and my physical and mental health, I likely wouldn't make it to a 4th year of teaching. Instead I would become a part of the nearly 50% of educators who leave the classroom in their first 5 years (Will, 2018).

Thus began the journey in search of efficient, effective ways to respond to student writing that has culminated in this book.

The first step in this journey was to assess the extent of the problem, so for several months I tracked the number of hours I spent hunched over student writing. I eventually came to an average of 10 hours per week, which falls in the middle of the range provided by the only research I know on the subject, a nearly 55-year-old study of high school English teachers who reported that they spend between 9 hours and 12 hours per week on average responding to student writing (Applebee, 1966).

While on the surface 10 hours might not seem overly oppressive, it is important to remember that those hours come *on top of everything else*. A study of 10,000 teachers by the Bill & Melinda Gates Foundation and Scholastic (2012) found that teachers work an average of 53 hours per week (p. 13). It is important to remember that 53 hours is the average, meaning many teachers work more than that. It is also important to note that the same study gets to 53 hours by allocating less than 2 hours per week to grading and responding to work, meaning many of those above the 53-hour mark are likely writing teachers who must shoulder the same demands that other teachers do *and* those extra hours with student writing. It's safe to assume that many of the teachers in this study even work well above the 60+-hours-per-week threshold where work becomes classified as a serious mental and physical health risk (Popomaronis, 2016). I know that at my 3-year mark, I certainly did.

Did You Know?

Did you know that regularly working 60+ hours comes with the following risks?

- A threefold increase in relationship problems
- A nearly 60% increase in cardiovascular issues
- Significantly higher rates of obesity, substance abuse, depression, and "all-around mortality"
- Reduced productivity (Popomaronis, 2016)

The amount of time I spent with papers was clearly a problem, but unfortunately the answer was not simply to assign less writing. My students—like most American students—were already struggling with writing far more and showing growth far slower than I'd like, and I had a suspicion that doing less writing wasn't going to help this. This left me with a really hard question: How could I help my students make significant progress in their writing—without burning myself out in the process? Or, in other words, how could I become more efficient *and* more effective in my writing instruction?

When I first really dug into these questions, the answers I came upon didn't make me feel any better either. So many of the *time-saving* techniques I encountered felt like the kinds of ineffective silver bullets that education is filled with—quick fixes that ultimately don't deliver on their lofty promises and hype. Further, many of the well-supported articles I read confirmed that the key to reversing the dismal long-standing student writing trends is that we need to do *more*—assign more writing, give more feedback, have more conferences . . . at this point the options in front of me were dismal and my hope started to flicker.

A Flash of Hope

As I continued to dig deeper, I did start to find some good news among this sea of scary statistics and troubling questions. Although we do need to do more in some respects of our writing instruction and can neither manufacture more hours in the day nor school budgets that will significantly lower our class sizes, there also exists a long history of amazing research-based practices that really can increase our effectiveness as writing instructors *while* decreasing the hours we work.

The key behind nearly all these is feedback—or the information that we provide to students concerning their work—and how, when, and how often we provide it. Feedback is the most time-consuming part of reading and responding to student papers. Most of us can read a paper in a couple minutes and give it a grade or assessment in a matter of seconds. It is our feedback that pushes the time needed to respond to a single paper to 10, 15, 20, or more minutes, and there are ways, grounded in research and already employed in real classrooms across the world, to provide strong feedback to our students throughout their writing process in a comparative flash.

Those practices are what this book is about. Over these five chapters, I hope to show you that it is possible to get out from under the mountains of papers while becoming a better writing teacher in the process.

Each chapter provides a different piece of the puzzle concerning how we can be better responders to student work in less time. The first two chapters focus on how we can work smarter, not harder, with the feedback we give. Chapter 1 dives deeply into efficiencies in an effort to divide the true gold—time-saving practices that really work—from the rampant and glittery fool's gold of quick fixes. Chapter 2 takes a close look at what makes feedback effective or ineffective, in the hopes that doing so will provide a path for which practices to jettison and that should be invested in.

The middle chapters detail what I call the multipliers, which are practices that dramatically increase the impact our feedback has on our students' writing. The goal with these is to enable writing teachers to give less feedback (thus saving time) yet have even more effect on how students learn, retain, and grow in

The Historic Struggle With Writing

To understand the extent that American students struggle with writing, it is worth looking at The Nation's Report Card on Writing (https://www.nationsreportcard.gov//), which has shown the same problem since the 1980s: Despite all the time we spend responding to writing, roughly three quarters of students leave 8th grade and 12th grade *without* being proficient in writing.

their writing. In Chapter 3 we look at how following a clear and consistent feedback cycle can encourage students to remember and adopt our feedback as their own; the ultimate goal of this is to get students revisiting each piece of feedback multiple times so that they squeeze every ounce of meaning from each word. Chapter 4 begins with an often overlooked fact: Feedback in a great many classrooms is the most consistent contact point between teachers and students and the source from which many students build their academic identities as writers, readers, thinkers, and students. This chapter examines how feedback can be used to build relationships and student academic identities without adding time to our responses, and how those relationships and identities can dramatically improve the efficacy of our feedback.

The final chapter provides a close examination of two often misunderstood education concepts: peer review and metacognition. The goal of this chapter is to understand how, by carefully scaffolding our students in peer review, we can increase the amount of meaningful feedback in our classes exponentially. Further, with training and practice in self-review, we can grow students' metacognition and refine their understanding of both their writing and our responses.

When one is offered more for less, it is wise to be wary. Likewise, faster is not always better. However, the right innovations can increase speed and allow us to do more with less. In 100 years Ford has gone from making a Model T every 2.5 minutes to making a cheaper and far superior new car every 4 seconds. Yet when it comes to giving feedback on student writing, the practices used today look an awful lot like they did when the first Model T rolled off the assembly line. For the sake of both our students and ourselves, it is past time for us to update how we respond to student work. And luckily for us, in those hundred years, amazing teachers and researchers have, often quietly, given us a blueprint for exactly how to do that. It is possible to respond to student writing effectively, efficiently, and memorably—in less time. Here's how.

Photo by Isabel Espinosa.

CHAPTER ONE

Giving Strong Feedback in Less Time
The Efficiencies

The very first article of the first issue of the *English Journal* from 1912 begins with a question: *Can good composition teaching be done under present conditions*? (see Figure 1.1). The current conditions the author was referring to? Having upward of 125 students under a teacher's care.

The author's answer? No, which he backs up by writing the following:

> Every year teachers resign, break down, perhaps become perma-
> nently invalided, having sacrificed ambition, health, and in not a
> few instances even life, in the struggle to do all the work expected of
> them. . . . Much money is spent, valuable teachers are worn out at an
> inhumanly rapid rate, and results are inadequate or wholly lacking.
> From any point of view—that of taxpayer, teacher, or pupil—such a
> situation is intolerable. (Hopkins, 1912)

One hundred and eight years later and the situation is equally intolerable. Results remain inadequate; teachers continue to be worn out at a rate that is not only inhuman but also increasing rapidly (Hackman & Morath, 2018); and the unacceptable level of 125 secondary students identified by the 1912 author would be a dream for many writing teachers, including this one, who currently has 159 students amongst his five classes.

THE ENGLISH JOURNAL

VOLUME I JANUARY 1912 NUMBER I

CAN GOOD COMPOSITION TEACHING BE DONE UNDER PRESENT CONDITIONS?[1]

EDWIN M. HOPKINS
University of Kansas

No.

This is a small and apparently unprotected word, occupying a somewhat exposed position; but it is upborne by indisputable truth.

FIGURE 1.1 • Not Much Has Changed in Over 100 Years

Consequently, when I first dug into the literature about ways to become more efficient, I discovered my struggle with the paper load was far from unique. Even the most renowned writing teachers bemoan the oppressive load that papers put on their shoulders. Carol Jago admits in her book *Papers, Papers, Papers* (2005) to having elaborate fantasies of driving to the ocean and consigning whole stacks of papers to the waves; Dr. Richard Haswell (2006), who has studied responses to papers for decades, calls them "the profession's mark of Cain" (p. 8); and Eric J. Mendelson (2018) recalls the iconic inscription on the gates of hell in Dante's *Inferno—Abandon all hope, ye who enter here*—when he gazes on a stack of papers.

I also learned that I was not the first to embark on some desperate and quixotic quest to improve my feedback while drastically cutting down the time it took. There is a colorful history of theories, systems, machines, and suggestions, all seeking or promising ways to be more effective and efficient. Sadly, many of them have been debunked, sit on a dubious research base, or are outright snake-oil. Yet among the noise, there are a number of practices created and curated by brilliant teachers that are widely supported by research and can actually help us grow more efficient and, at the same time, more effective, largely because they simplify our messages or eliminate the clutter. I've organized the most significant of these into seven time-saving tenets that can help us give strong feedback in less time:

1. Don't Read and Respond to Every Paper

2. Use More Targeted Feedback

3. Wait Until October to "Give" Grades/Assessments

4. Be a Teacher, Not an Editor

5. Go Digital

6. Automate *Some* Parts

7. Get in the Feedback Mindset

Time-Saving Tenet #1: Don't Read and Respond to Every Paper

As a new teacher I made sure to read every syllable my students wrote for my classes. While part of this was because I wanted to read what they wrote, I also did this because *not* reading something made me anxious. Deep down I worried that if my eyes didn't pass over a piece, somehow the students wouldn't learn from it, as if my gaze was the necessary catalyst to begin the learning process. I also feared that students wouldn't take an ungraded assignment seriously or follow my directions. After all, by the time they reach my secondary classroom, a great many students have learned that the reason to write is primarily to get a grade.

Even now, to not read or respond to student work still often feels like cutting a corner, but limiting what we read and respond to is actually one of the most responsible things a writing teacher can do. There are two key reasons for this:

(1) To maximize their learning, students need to write for sustained amounts of time every day—30 minutes to 60 minutes according to many experts (National Center for Education Statistics, 2012; Cruz, 2015).

(2) Students need spaces where they can play with writing, try new things, and take the necessary risks needed to maximize their growth.

When we try to read and assess all writing, we stand in the way of these best practices. There is no way for a teacher to read 30 minutes to 60 minutes of writing from 159 students every day. Trying to do so courts burnout or makes it more likely that the teacher will eventually limit the amount of writing she assigns in an effort to keep up. Additionally, many students won't take risks or try new things when they know the teacher's watchful gaze will be on them. In these situations, a teacher's eyes will potentially slow and obstruct learning rather than being a catalyst.

Instead, it is important that our students engage in lots of exploratory writing where they write even though the writing will go unread and uncommented on by the teacher. This type of writing can be powerful in many situations, but it works especially well when students are writing to

- Learn content
- Collect their thoughts
- Consolidate knowledge
- Learn about themselves
- Generate thinking
- Practice a new skill

These types of exploratory writing are about learning, creating, and changing. Those things happen best when we set aside our need to be competent and correct, because our first attempts to wield new ideas, skills, and approaches are generally clumsy and littered with missteps. Doing that is difficult for a lot of students when they know that their teacher will be watching. Many students have had at least one negative experience with teachers looking at their work, as a student shared with me last year:

Common Exploratory Writing

- Journals
- Free or quick writes
- Blogs
- Reflections
- Note taking
- Summaries
- Writing on graphic organizers
- Outlines

> In third grade we were writing journals and I misspelled Michigan. I remember the teacher saying to the class, with me standing right there, how ridiculous it is not to know how to spell my state. "Class, how do you spell *Michigan*," she continued, and everybody recited M-I-C-H-I-G-A-N. . . . I was really embarrassed and have remembered since.

This student remembered this experience from 8 years earlier so clearly that he switched to present tense for part of it as he told it to me. If we add up even a few moments like this, it helps explain why many students look at a teacher reading their paper like surfers look at a dorsal fin approaching as they sit in open water.

Also, it should be mentioned that students who've been embarrassed by teachers aren't the only ones who react with trepidation when the teacher will be looking at their writing. I've found the students who are often the most nervous about teachers are often those with the highest grades or those who really like a class or teacher. For them, even the smallest assignment is often a serious potential threat because it could do damage to their GPAs or the *perfect* images they have carefully cultivated within the class.

Consequently, we need to allow as many moments as possible where our students can, in the words of Kelly Gallagher (2006), "get out from under the shadow of the red pen" (p. 143). We need to give them plenty of safe harbors where they can stumble, play, practice, and learn far away from teachers' pens of any color. Doing this doesn't mean that we abdicate our responsibility to respond to student work, either; we will be looking at it soon enough. Instead, it just means that before we look at it we will give students time to develop and refine their new skills, ideas, and creations before we move on to the business of giving them feedback.

If you are still unsure of stepping back from reading and responding to all writing in your classroom, think about it a different way: In no other pursuit—ranging from painting to playing piano to shooting baskets—do we feel that every minute of practice should be observed and commented on by a teacher or coach. In those, we rightly identify that students need space and lots of practice. This is why the best music schools ring with far more notes than any instructor could ever process and the best diving practices have more flips and twists than any coach could ever see. It is also why writing classrooms should produce far more words than even the most efficient and diligent writing teacher could ever hope to read.

Will Students Take Writing Seriously if I Don't Grade It?

Although there is much more talk about purpose, mindsets, credibility, and relationships in the upcoming chapters—and all these can act as motivators when grades and teacher glares go away—I face far less trouble with students doing ungraded writing pieces in class than graded ones, especially once I explain to them why I won't be reading the piece. Once students realize what it means to be given space to follow their interests and ideas away from the teacher's eyes, most students, including a surprisingly high number of self-classified nonwriters, engage more with a piece and work longer on it than they would have if I had attached points.

An Important Detail
About Not Reading Student Work

In many states, teachers are required by law to report information they have concerning student abuse, self-harm, and violence. And even in states where mandatory reporting laws aren't strong, teachers—and writing teachers in particular—are, in the words of Douglas Fisher and Nancy Frey (2018), the "eyes and ears of the mental health system." For these reasons, it is incredibly important that we are very clear with our students from the beginning about what we will and won't be reading. Being coy about the pieces we will read can open up legal trouble for a teacher who doesn't read something that should be reported. Even more importantly, it can also lead to missing student admissions of danger—admissions that if students put in writing, they wanted you to see. For more information on mandatory reporting, www.childwelfare.gov has a host of wonderful resources and links.

Time-Saving Tenet #2: Use More Targeted Feedback

Two things we know very clearly about feedback is that it has the biggest impact when it is

- Given regularly (Farrington et al., 2012, p. 36)
- Received as soon as possible by the students (McGee, 2017, p. 20)

It makes a lot of sense that regular feedback given shortly after a task is completed would have a larger impact than intermittent feedback received weeks later, yet in most classes the latter is far more common than the former. This is because when feedback comes exclusively in time-intensive scribbling through the margins of papers—the standard and only feedback mechanism for a great many classes—it will inevitably be significantly delayed and intermittent.

If we want to get feedback to students regularly and quickly, we need to begin utilizing other, faster forms of feedback in the place of some of those extensive margin notes. Useful feedback can be given in a multitude of ways to a multitude of different writing assignments and moments in the writing process, after all.

This book looks at these different ways and times to give feedback (including margin notes), but I want to start with the one that I use the most often—targeted feedback—which is feedback focused specifically on helping students build or refine a certain skill. Targeted feedback works so well because when we focus solely on one skill, our feedback can be both meaningful and fast, often given by the next day or even within the class period itself. This speed also allows us to give feedback much more regularly, which a University of Chicago literature review argued as "[an essential practice] for creating a school or classroom culture where success is perceived as possible" (Farrington et al., 2012, p. 38).

To see targeted feedback in action, consider this assignment from a unit I teach on commas, colons, semicolons, and dashes (see Figure 1.2 for an example; you can download this and much more from the companion website at **resources.corwin.com/flashfeedback).**

Punctuation Write

Please write a one-page, double-spaced paper in the genre of your choice and on the topic of your choice. Somewhere in the paper you should correctly and thoughtfully use the following punctuation:

- At least two dashes
- At least two colons
- At least two semicolons
- At least four different types of commas

The grade will be earned purely on the usage of this punctuation. Here is the rubric:

Criteria	Points Possible	Points Earned
Thoughtful and correct use of at least two dashes. No dashes are misused.	2	____
Thoughtful and correct use of at least two colons. No colons are misused.	2	____
Thoughtful and correct use of at least two semicolons. No semicolons are misused.	2	____
Thoughtful and correct use of all commas; four different types of commas are used; no commas are misused	4	____

FIGURE 1.2 • Targeted Writing Assignment—Punctuation

This assignment generally comes after the students have gotten pretty comfortable with these punctuation marks, meaning my goals when I assign this are to

- Assess each student's understanding of these punctuation marks
- Redirect any students who have misconceptions about any particular mark

When it comes to responding to this assignment, I keep my eyes fixed on these goals, and my responses focus solely on assessing punctuation usage and clearing up misconceptions. By keeping my feedback targeted, I can read and respond to an entire class-set in well under half an hour by following this process:

1. If I want to return this type of targeted assignment in the same class period, I schedule it before an established block of drafting and/or reading time. This is important because while my responses will be fast, they won't be instantaneous, and I don't want students sitting around waiting for me. My rule for students in these situations is simple: Once students finish the assignment, they roll right into the reading or writing.

2. When students finish, they share their paper with me via a Google Doc, and I quickly scan each paper using the find function (Command-F) to highlight the elements (colon, semicolon, dash, commas) that I'm looking for. If students are writing by hand, an alternative to the find function is to have them highlight or underline each time they use a comma, colon, semicolon, and dash. The whole idea is that as the one assessing them, I can use these visual markers to help me instantly find the targeted areas, allowing me to move at maximum speed.

3. I then fill out the rubric with the points earned. In doing that, I simply take away one point for each misused comma, colon, semicolon, or dash. If a student has no errors, I give them full points and quickly move on. Because my secondary goal is to help redirect any misconceptions about the punctuation marks, if a student does have an error or issue, I will highlight the error, too. I do not fix the errors because doing this takes more time and is not ideal for learning because I would be the one doing the work, not the student.

4. Finally, I require students who made errors to fix them. I generally strive to give students class time to revise and the opportunity to regain all lost points, because I have found that this added incentive, time, and access to me are key if I want students to move forward in earnest. As I mentioned

above, I also don't make the changes for them, as I want them to go through the internal grappling that is necessary to learning something at a deep level. Of course, I do provide resources for them to find the right answers. They can access the resources from class (visit the companion website at **resources.corwin .com/flashfeedback** to see the punctuation tutorials available to them), conference with partners, and come to me if they have exhausted other resources and are still stumped.

A Class Without Grades?

In most corners of our education system, writing, feedback, and grades are inextricably linked. This can be problematic at times because it is well-documented that grades can have some pretty negative effects on writing, identity, and feedback. They can damage the attention paid to feedback (more on that in Chapter 2), make students more risk averse, and have a negative impact on intrinsic motivation.

Still, grades are largely nonnegotiable in the educational climate of today. For example, my contract states very clearly that new grades need to be put into the online gradebook weekly. I've also found how and how often teachers grade to be a very personal matter, and it is worth mentioning that reasonable arguments exist both for a variety of approaches to grading or going gradeless. Considering these things, this book doesn't take a stand for or against using grades, and many examples and resources do have points associated with them for use by teachers who assign grades. That being said, it might be worth some time to look into the interesting experiments being undertaken across this country by innovative educators who are *going gradeless*. Often, even if we keep grades, we can incorporate useful bits and pieces from these gradeless laboratories. Some of the most interesting places to go to learn about going gradeless include

- The Paper Graders: www.thepapergraders.org
- Teachers Going Gradeless: www.teachersgoinggradeless.com
- *Hacking Assessment: 10 Ways to Go Gradeless in a Traditional Grades School* by Starr Sackstein (2015)
- *Shift This!: How to Implement Gradual Changes for MASSIVE Impact in Your Classroom* by Joy Kirr (2017)

Targeted feedback comes with many advantages. It allows for more consistent and timely feedback while also adding little or ideally nothing to the paper load that I take home with me. With this assignment, even in my biggest classes, the students can do it, get timely personal and meaningful feedback, and revise if needed within the confines of class time. Also, even though I write nothing, the feedback is focused and clear. Students know exactly what I expect them to do, what they got right, and what they missed, and the results are often stunning. One or two targeted assignments such as this can move the needle on something like comma or colon usage more than I used to see in an entire year of putting corrections and comments in the margins of larger and more globally assessed polished writing pieces.

Time-Saving Tenet #3:
Wait Until October to "Give" Grades

I used to assign a full polished essay in the first week of school to give me a sense of each student's writing skills. The problems with this though were threefold:

1. I had 150+ papers to read and assess by the end of the first week, putting me under a pile of papers before the year had really even begun.

2. I hadn't taught the students anything yet, meaning that if I graded their writing, I was largely grading them on what they had learned before my class.

3. The grades I assigned would set each student up as A, B, C, or D student from the very start. Getting a big grade early in the class can solidify in a student a fixed mindset that corresponds to the grade received.

I now strive to not grade anything until well into October. This is a notion that I adapted from Kelly Gallagher's (2006) *Teaching Adolescent Writers*:

When I coached high school basketball early in my career, I wanted my students to get as much practice as possible throughout the week so that they would be ready for the game on Friday night. . . . It would have been crazy to just ask them to show up for the game Friday night without first giving my players a place to practice (the gym) and a lot of time to develop their skills (daily practices). . . . If we are going to require students to write complex essays, we need to give them the necessary time to develop their writing skills. They should be "messing around" and "playing" with writing every day to lay the foundation for the more challenging writing assignments that lie ahead. (p. 31)

Those first weeks of the school year are a necessary time for students to mess around, play, and practice writing. Of course, I am required to put in grades, so my gradebook doesn't sit empty during those weeks. Students get plenty of grades, but the grades are based on effort, meeting deadlines, or smaller targeted assignments, with the larger pieces and their corresponding bigger and more global grades waiting until students have put in plenty of practice and playing.

I have found this approach to be good for both the students and for me. It gives them a chance—even in a class with grades—to play and practice and develop writing identities that don't have a grade at the center. And for me it frees up time to focus on setting up my classes, deal with those beginning-of-the-year extras such as curriculum night and conferences, and get other work out of the way so when responding to polished writing does eventually come, I have more headspace to manage it.

This rhythm of beginning with lots of ungraded and targeted writing before embarking on larger papers is how my year starts, but this pattern isn't something that goes away once the weather grows cold. It is instead a rhythm my class has the entire year, repeating with each new unit. I like to think about each unit in the way that Dave Stuart Jr. (2017) frames it, as a "Pyramid of Writing Priorities." The foundation of this pyramid (shown in Figure 1.3) is that any new unit should be built on daily ungraded and unread *practice writing*; the next level is weekly *targeted writing*, where students get regular, quick feedback from the teacher concerning the key concepts throughout the unit; and the top level is *polished writing*, where after lots of practice and targeted writing, students create longer revised pieces that incorporate all the lessons from the unit.

Few changes I've made to my teaching have been as significant in a positive way for both the students and me. The students get clearly defined places to practice and time to build skills before worrying about "bigger" grades, and I get large sections of the calendar year where I didn't have huge stacks of polished papers weighing down my bag and my psyche.

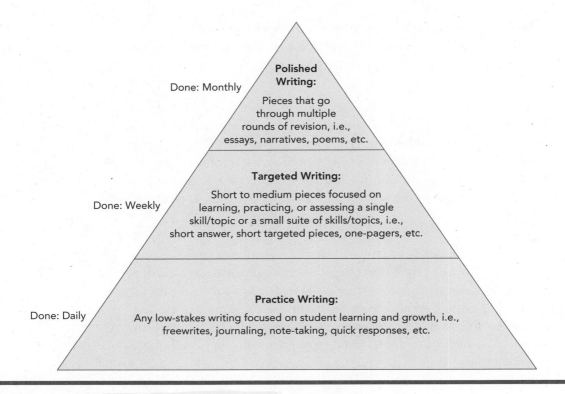

FIGURE 1.3 • The Pyramid of Writing Priorities

Time-Saving Tenet #4:
Be a Teacher, Not an Editor

In her landmark essay "Responding to Student Writing," Nancy Sommers (1982) suggests that there exists an "unwritten canon" passed from teacher to teacher about how we are supposed to respond to student writing. The chief rule at the heart of the canon is that teachers should *correct* each paper as an editor would by filling the margins with a large number of quick, curt comments and corrections concerning every error they see.

> "We have no right to scatter a barrage of messages across the landscape of a student's paper when we're trying to teach concepts like focus and control." –Muriel Harris (1979) in "The Overgraded Paper"

Sommers is critical of this approach for many reasons. Its haste may lead to a terse tone from the teacher that can intimidate students. The relative brevity of each comment does little to differentiate the minor concerns from the major ones. The quickly scrawled comments often lead to confusion. But her most damning criticism—one that has been echoed by nearly every writing expert over the last 35 years—is that it is simply ineffective.

To understand the reason why this approach often leads to little or no learning, let's think about how our brains work. In *Why Don't Students Like School?* Daniel Willingham (2010b) states that "[m]emory is the residue of thought," (p. 41), in other words, our brains aren't just empty receptacles waiting to have knowledge poured into them. Instead, because we only have space to store a fraction of what we encounter on a daily basis, our brains are more like an armed fortress with guards stopping to interrogate every would-be piece of information before it is admitted into the halls of memory. What information is admitted to memory depends on how much attention we *pay* to it. If we don't spend much time thinking about and grappling with something, the brain generally deems it unlikely to matter and tags it as something that does not need to be remembered. If we do spend time thinking through and grappling with something, though, the brain realizes it is probably worth remembering and might even be worth understanding, and thus begins the process of memorization and learning.

Most teachers understand the foundational roles attention and thinking play in learning when designing lessons, so we keep the number of learning objectives modest so that students have time to think through each. But when commenting on papers the opposite is often true. Instead of granting space, teachers often cram dozens of distinct lessons into each page of student writing. If this seems like an exaggeration, take a look at Figure 1.4, which shows corrections I made on an essay many years ago when I was still commenting on everything I noticed.

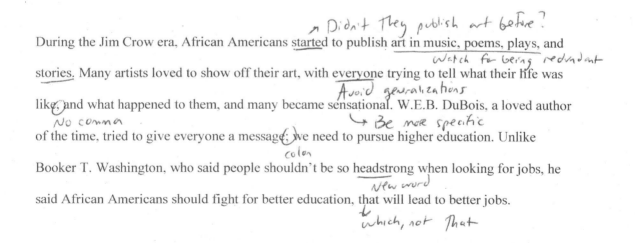

FIGURE 1.4 • Too Many Comments for a Student's Brain to Focus!

At first glance, the comments might not look overly oppressive, yet in this seven-line excerpt, we see five comments covering five distinctly different writing lessons—redundancy, generalizations, clarity, accuracy, and word choice—and four corrections delivered to the student in rapid, staccato statements. A two-page paper with that same rate would have over 35 comments and 30 corrections, potentially addressing 30, 40, or 50 distinctly different concepts. Thinking about that many lessons long enough to truly understand and internalize them would take most students months or even years, yet here I expected the student to do it in a single revision.

Further, when teachers comment on every passing thought and observation as they work through a paper, they are more likely to confuse or scare students away from learning any of them. In my earlier years when I used to fill student papers with comments, I found that many students grew so overwhelmed by the cognitive task of working through a paper filled to the brim with problems that they simply did not engage. Instead they found the nearest trash can and made short work of the papers I had spent long hours correcting. Even more concerning is that the students most likely to disregard a paper full of comments are the students who struggle the most with writing (Crisp, 2007), and with every set of ignored comments the gap between them and their classmates tends to grow even larger.

The solution to this problem of over-response is one of the rare simple and straightforward win-wins in the complicated story of responding to writing: We need to make fewer comments, often significantly fewer. By ignoring the urge to play an editor who marks everything, we reclaim our role as teachers. At this point, we can do what good teachers do—namely, assess the situation, prioritize what the students really need to learn right now, create clear and thoughtful lessons, and then give students the time and space to learn those lessons.

Further, not only do fewer comments paradoxically lead to more learning, but by cutting down the number of comments we give, we save *a lot* of time. If a teacher commented at the pace I did on that essay and thus averaged 35 comments per paper and that teacher had my 159 students, the total number of comments made would be 5,565 for one round of essays alone (it is worth noting this doesn't even include the corrections). Cut that in half and assume an average of 15 seconds per comment, and the nearly 2,800 comments eliminated will save 11.5 hours. Imagine the myriad places that time could be reinvested,

The Scale of Writing Concerns: The 4 Ds

Chapter 2 discusses in greater detail how the topics we discuss in feedback should match the needs of the student, but a good rule of thumb is to mark like a teacher. This means only mark as much as the students can actually learn and focus on the areas of highest need. For my part, while there is no one progression of writing instruction that has been proven to work perfectly for every student, there is a scale of concerns that I keep in mind when deciding what I will comment on. When reviewing student writing, I ask myself: Is this a destructive, detracting, distracting, or delivery issue?

Area of Highest Priority: Destructive Issues. A destructive issue is anything so damaging to the clarity or credibility of the piece that it essentially outweighs any other positives the paper may have, such as no punctuation or paragraphing, bizarre formatting, or a wildly off-target tone.

Next Highest Priority: Detracting Issues. A detracting issue is any that takes a significant amount away from the reading experience. Examples of detracting issues are major organizational issues, lots of unclear language, or significant word misusage.

Next Highest Priority: Distracting Issues. A distracting issue is something that hurts the reading experience for a brief moment. An incorrectly formatted quote, wooden dialogue in a narrative, and generalizations or redundancies are all examples of issues that often would be seen as distracting issues.

Lowest Level Priority: Delivery Issues. A delivery issue is one where the delivery could be stronger than it is. Delivery issues tend to be things like word choice, sentence structure, use of literary and rhetorical devices, and overuse of linking verbs such as *to be*.

It is important to remember that this is a rough guideline, not a polished rule. Also, the categories can be fluid. Sometimes linking verbs or sentence structure can significantly detract from a paper while tone or organizational issues don't always seriously damage a piece. Also, sometimes we might comment on things such as a student's effort or growth. Still, thinking through the impact the issues have on the reader usually helps me know what to tackle now and what to focus on at a later date.

ranging from improving the depth and clarity of the feedback we do give to giving yourself more of those essential nights where you put the papers away to spend time with family, friends, or long-neglected hobbies.

Time-Saving Tenet #5: Go Digital

I am a Luddite in so many ways. I don't own an e-reader, I am seemingly always at the copy machine in my school, and you can count the number of web tools I use in my classroom on one hand. I find that while we so often proclaim technology a universal savior, there are plenty of places where it can be an unnecessary complication that detracts from the core work of the classroom—namely reading, writing, and thinking.

The one area where I am utterly convinced that technology is an unequivocal upgrade, though, is in providing efficient feedback to students. When I respond to student papers in writing, I exclusively do it digitally. I encourage you to do the same, if possible, because the reasons for going digital are compelling:

- The *average* person's typing speed is faster than the *theoretical maximum* speed one could reach for writing by hand (Griffiths, 2015). Based on the research, it would be fair to assume that most seasoned keyboardists can type twice as fast as they could write by hand. This means twice as much feedback in the same amount of time.

- Like plenty of English teachers, my handwriting is far from perfect, especially after an hour of giving feedback. When I used to give feedback by hand, one or two students inevitably came to me for clarification concerning what I said—and those were just the students who were brave enough to approach me. With digital comments, there is no chance of the students not being able to read any of the comments.

- Students can access our digital comments instantly and in perpetuity. This allows us to get them the feedback faster and allows them to revisit it later, which is very useful for everything from putting together portfolios to creating reflections.

- Digital comments allow us to link mentor texts and resources (more on this in a bit).

- Any modern word processing program allows teachers to view the "Version/Comment History" to see the full history of every single keystroke that stems from each piece of feedback. Before I commented digitally, I always wondered what my students did with my comments. Now I know. Also, I can revisit each comment I give through the "Version/Comment History." This is super useful because, among the blur of my feedback to my 159 students, I rarely remember what comment I gave to what student. Digital feedback allows us, for example, to make sure that we don't praise students for "taking a good step" when they haven't done any significant revisions. It also helps me repeat the points I want to repeat, ensures that I don't repeat the points I don't want to repeat, and generally provides more accurate information when I talk to students about their evolution as writers.

Time-Saving Tenet #6: Automate *Some* Parts

One of the oldest and most common suggestions for how to give feedback more efficiently are correction codes. The idea behind these is pretty simple: We have a lot of students who share similar issues in their writing, and thus we find ourselves writing similar comments over and over and over. With correction codes, the teacher, in an effort to save time and sanity, creates a shorthand for common comments and suggestions and a key that helps the students decode the shorthand. (For example, WW indicates "wrong word," SP indicates a spelling error, M indicates a missing word, "?" indicates a lack of clarity, and so forth.)

Then, whenever the teacher needs to give one of those common responses, she can just write the code and move on, ultimately saving a lot of time.

This practice likely comes from copy editors have been using coded shorthand squiggles forever because they save a lot of time. Imagine how much faster it is to just put a series of letters and symbols instead of writing carefully composed sentences. Similarly, many products for writing teachers dating back decades claim that by exclusively using their codes a teacher can read and respond to a full essay in 5 minutes or less.

These approaches might sound great on the surface, but there is one major problem with them: We are not copy editors—we are teachers—and in the context of teaching, correction codes often have a number of negative effects on students, with some of the biggest being:

- Their one one-size-fits-all nature often makes responses based on codes feel cold, impersonal, or aloof.

- Because the language of the code isn't specifically aimed at the student, there is a much higher likelihood that students will misunderstand some of it.

- When teacher comments are predominantly codes, a relationship is established in which the teacher is the all-knowing judge and the student the chronically flawed novice—a serious problem I discuss more deeply in the Chapter 2.

- And most problematic, codes can train students to think that revision is less about taking a close, hard look at a piece than it is about playing a game of whack-a-mole for the errors identified on the correction code sheet.

These downsides are the likely reason that while correction codes have been around as long as writing teachers, they remain relatively rare in practicing classrooms. Most writing teachers I know would love to give feedback to an essay in 5 minutes and many have flirted with codes at some point, but few use them in any serious way. Likewise, I found my own experiments with highly coded feedback ultimately unsatisfying because the negative impact on my students, who seemed to grow less engaged in their writing and the classroom, overshadowed any time saved.

This history of codes is important to understand because it makes clear the dangers of overly automating our feedback. At the same time the idea of automating *some* rote elements of feedback isn't a bad idea. Too often, we throw out an entire idea because some parts of it don't work, but there are some areas where automation can streamline and even improve our responses to student work *without* the negative side effects. Here are some I have found to be the most effective.

TARGETED FEEDBACK FOR TARGETED WRITING

Targeted writing works best when students receive fast feedback, because the whole goal is to give students stepping stones that move them toward success on the larger polished pieces. This is why, when I assign targeted writing, I respond to it in short and quick ways. For example, when I give the targeted punctuation example assignment earlier in the chapter, I simply highlight the errors, because this is fast and yet still clear. In other targeted writes, the quick feedback will take different forms. I do a short targeted write focused on word choice where I put stars next to my favorite word choice examples to celebrate the students' successes, and when I do a targeted writing assignment that focuses on building paraphrasing skills, I mark "PP" next to any segment where the paraphrasing runs too close to the original, putting them in danger of "Potential Plagiarism." To see these targeted writing and feedback examples and many more, please go to **resources.corwin.com/flashfeedback**.

This shorthand approach is similar to correction codes in that it allows me to pass along information quickly—often in real time—which is super important in the early stages of skill building. Where it differs is that I only do it in targeted writes that focus on just one or two things; when it comes to larger papers, my responses are much more human and organic. I've found that this pairing of quick, shorthand feedback to targeted writes and regular deeper, personalized responses to students' polished writing saves time without the negative side effects that result when codes are the only responses that a teacher gives.

A CAN OF COMMENTS

No student paper is the same, but there are some issues that are both highly common and incredibly hard to explain in a clear, succinct manner. For these specific issues, I have found it useful to have a canned explanation ready that I can then take and *adapt* for the student. Consider, for example, the comma splice. To truly explain what a comma splice is, one also needs to discuss

- dependent and independent clauses,
- conjunctions,

- comma placement, and
- why they matter.

This is not something that can be done in a brief sentence. Here is the most succinct, yet human and comprehensive explanation I've been able to come up with:

> I notice that you have a lot of comma splices. These are where you join two phrases using just a comma, which technically makes the sentence a run-on. Here is an example of another run-on with a comma splice: "I read *Harry Potter*, I loved it!" To correctly use a comma here, you need to use a **comma and a conjunction**, for example: "I read *Harry Potter*, **and** I loved it!" You can also break it into two sentences. The best way to test for comma splices is whenever you come to a comma, look to the right and left of it. If each side of the comma (like "I read *Harry Potter*" and "I loved it!") could be a complete sentence, then you want to use a comma **and** a conjunction (such as and/but/or) to connect the two parts. Here is a link to a sheet that has some examples, if you need further guidance.

As a high school English teacher, I come across a nearly endless stream of comma splices early in the year, and to rewrite something to that effect for each one would take a very long time. Consequently, I have a handful of common comments that I keep in a comment bank to use in those specialized situations. (I use the Google Comment Bank in Google Classroom, but if you don't have Google Classroom, storing the comments in a Comment Bank Word Document would work, too.)

I don't believe there is anything wrong with occasional usage of canned comments in these types of situations, though it is important to remember that even well-crafted canned comments might feel, well, canned, which can turn students off. So it's important to adapt each comment to the student in front of me regarding

- **The Terminology.** If we think about comma splices, some students will be comfortable with grammatical terms like *independent clause, dependent clause, phrase,* and *conjunction* while for others these phrases may as well be ancient Greek. This means for some I will use these terms, for others I will teach these terms, and for others I teach around that terminology because

I don't want to overload them (for instance, see how I avoid discussing independent and dependent clauses in the comma splice comment above but don't shy away from terms like *conjunction* and *phrase*).

- **The Approach**. Different approaches will speak to different students. If I am worried that a college-bound, second-semester senior might not care about comma splices due to "senioritis," I might tell him about the professor who handed a paper back to me during my freshman year at college and told me he would grade it once I learned what a comma splice was. If I am worried that a student will take her comma splices as a sign she is bad at grammar, I will find some way to offer kind words of support surrounding places she used commas correctly.

Also, when using these canned comments, I remain vigilant about staying in teaching mode, not editing mode. In other words, it's important to limit the number of canned comments so we don't overload our students. I strive to not deploy more than two canned comments per paper, and I only use them when the topic is something I was planning on focusing on anyway.

LINKED RESOURCES

This idea from Catlin Tucker (2013) spoke to me instantly because hyperlinking to things is a really useful part of the grammar of the blogging world where my writing about education began. Whenever a blogger has a concept that readers might need more information about, we add a hyperlink to ferry the reader directly to a relevant resource. I do this all the time when I blog, and now I do it to save time when I respond to student writing.

Similar to my can of comments, I have a file of saved mentor texts and tutorials that I hyperlink in students' writing to provide an example, inspiration, or more information. If they're not writing online, I also make available printed versions of these resources.

As with comments, I deploy these hyperlinks sparingly; once again, too many can overload students in the same way that too many comments can. And I am careful not to send the same students the same links over and over because

> ## Got comments?
>
> The companion website at **resources .corwin.com/flashfeedback** provides a list of hyperlinks that allow you to access my can of comments bank, including student-friendly explanations for
>
> - Comma splices
> - Issues with sentence-length variation
> - Overuse of linking verbs, and specifically *to be*
> - Run-ons and fragments
> - Apostrophes
> - Paraphrasing and plagiarism
> - Transition issues
> - Dull word choice

eventually that could insinuate that I am not paying close attention to their writing. But in the right situations, these links can allow me to give much deeper feedback with just a few seconds of work.

USE RUBRICS (WELL)

In her book *Rethinking Rubrics*, Maja Wilson (2006) explains that the modern rubric arose in response to the democratization of education. As the numbers of citizens allowed into upper levels of education swelled, colleges needed a way to differentiate between candidates. Rubrics specifically rose to prominence in the 1960s as a way to organize the notoriously disorderly branch of academia that is writing into *core* components that could then be rated and ranked. Wilson points out that they did impose a sort of order, but they also had the unintentional consequence of turning writing for many students into an activity in checking off boxes on the rubric and turning many teachers toward more formulaic writing instruction.

As a practicing teacher, I have seen this happen with rubrics many times. Rubrics are a tempting concrete landmark for both teachers and students to fix their gaze upon, and if poorly constructed, they can indeed warp the writing process into something that resembles box-checking. However, I don't think rubrics should be cast out; instead, we should use rubrics as tools that come only *after* thoughtful, coherent instruction, not as stand-ins for thoughtful, coherent instruction (Jago, 2005).

Like canned comments, rubrics thoughtfully deployed can act as tools to provide fast, effective feedback. In general, rubrics are most useful for smaller assignments where you want the students to engage in closed learning objectives, which are learning objectives with relatively clear yes or no answers. (We delve in Chapters 2 and 3 into using rubrics for assessing larger, polished pieces.) Some examples of closed learning objectives include

- Did you use that comma correctly?
- Are your topic sentences clear?
- Do you correctly use at least two metaphors?
- Is your use of parallel structure correct? And does it bring emphasis to key moments?

While wrinkles and caveats can apply to each question, in general they can be answered in the affirmative or negative, making them perfect for rubrics and their corresponding boxes.

Figure 1.5 shows an example of a rubric I use for an assignment I give in the relatively early stages of teaching students about persuasive techniques.

This rubric comes when students are building their surface knowledge of these persuasive tools, making it a perfect moment for the basic binary questions that rubrics allow us to answer in a flash. Generally, I will fill in the boxes with a simple yes or no, putting comments only when a necessary point needs to be made. While I recognize that advanced use of parallel structure or pathos is hard

TECHNIQUE	HOW IT IS OFTEN USED	DO YOU USE IT IN A WAY THAT SHOWS UNDERSTANDING?
Rhetorical Questions	Rhetorical questions are often meant to get the audience thinking about a larger topic without feeling like you are trying to persuade them.	Yes / No
Generalization	Authors often use generalization when they want their audience to feel connected to something larger.	Yes / No
Parallel Structure	Parallel structure is meant to give added weight and an epic feel to something. It is often best deployed in the "big moments."	Yes / No
Symbolism	Humans are symbolic creatures. Having potent symbols where something represents something else (e.g., storm clouds often are symbols for coming trouble) can often help in adding depth and emotion to an argument.	Yes / No
Pathos	Humans are also emotional creatures. Pathos is where you seek to persuade by evoking strong emotions.	Yes / No

FIGURE 1.5 • Persuasive Technique Rubric

to talk about in this same yes or no format, in the early stages, when I just want to give students a fast thumbs up or down on whether they are using each device correctly, rubrics prove an invaluable tool. They help students move quickly through these early stages and toward more advanced uses of these techniques on larger polished pieces.

Time-Saving Tenet #7:
Get in the Feedback Mindset

It is easy to develop a somewhat antagonistic or outright toxic relationship with a stack of student writing, either in paper or online, waiting for a response. The amount of time and mental energy student writing demands and the icky feelings that can come with assigning grades to students can make it feel like a chore that has to be endured. I've been there. I've had more than a few moments where I resented the stacks sitting in front of me and weighing on my psyche and ignored them for weeks because I just didn't have it in me to start in on them.

Feedback is taxing emotional and cognitive work, so these feelings are normal, but I would also argue that the moments when I felt this way—when I felt my students' papers were enemies, not opportunities—I probably read them slower, procrastinated more, and generally gave feedback that was less effective.

These days, I strive to stay in the right mindset when I'm reading and responding to student work, because that mindset ultimately equals better work in less time. Here are some of the things I've found that help me stay in that positive frame of mind.

CREATE POSITIVE GRADING ROUTINES

In her book *Grit*, Angela Duckworth (2016) explains that one of the main ways that successful professional athletes and authors regularly do seemingly more than other people is through establishing thoughtful rituals and routines. Duckworth refers to routines as "godsends," because once we establish them, the thorniest tasks just become a daily part of life, like doing laundry or brushing teeth (p. 139). How does Michael Phelps swim 100,000 yards a week? How does Warren Buffett read 6 hours a day? The answer boils down to habitual routines, which help us get down to business at a specific time instead of wasting time wondering when we will get down to business (and often seeking plenty of distractions along the way).

For my part, for many years I played a sort of game where I weighed my paper stacks against the rest of the items on my to-do list. Generally, the papers lost and were nudged to some later, unspecified date. This deferral produced a momentary relief, but when I did finally engage with papers, it was weeks or, during a few rough semesters, months later, long after the window where the feedback would do much good.

I now take a page from Duckworth, Phelps, and Buffett and have blocked out paper-responding time each week. I always preface these blocks with a positive treat—my afternoon cup of coffee or a hot chocolate in the winter—and do them in the same spot with the same pen. Those little details might seem like overkill, but the research surrounding routines is clear that context often makes or breaks them (Clear, 2018). By surrounding my paper response with little cues, it is much more likely I won't give in to those minor distractions of checking Facebook or reading the news that can add up to major losses in time. Also, by building a treat into that time, my response sessions have become in some ways the most pleasant hours of my week. They are regular, quiet, efficient, have some indulgences, and best of all, they keep my stacks of papers small.

PLAN PAPERS

I used to assign, collect, and stack papers without any real plan. In my mind, I simply didn't have time to plan that, *too*. Sometimes the stars aligned and I wouldn't overload myself. Other times I'd find myself with hundreds of papers sitting on my desk, unsure of how to view those piles as anything but an onerous chore.

I now carefully plan when papers come back and when I will return them in the same way that I carefully plan a unit or the pages I assign in a novel. I actually have a calendar just for this. That calendar keeps me organized, which in turn keeps my physical and digital stacks small and me out of the crisis mindset that inevitably comes from piles of papers in need of my attention. Figure 1.6 shows a view of my calendar, to give you an idea of how I plan. Notice how each week has something that needs feedback. By planning it carefully, the stacks stay more moderately sized, which helps me keep on relatively good terms with them.

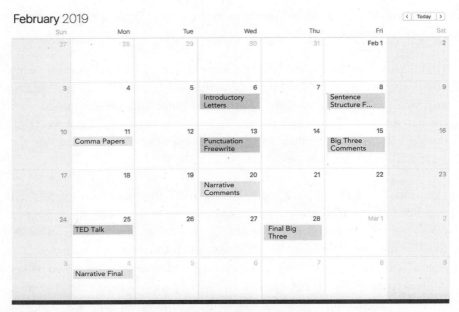

FIGURE 1.6 • Using a simple calendar I plan what types of feedback will be happening throughout a month and school year.

DON'T MIX BUSINESS WITH PLEASURE

When students pack up when I'm discussing homework or insist on having their phones sit next to them, I quietly remind them that the vast majority of humans share two traits:

1. We are terrible at multitasking.

2. We are even worse at realizing how bad we are at multitasking.

These are both true because our attention is limited. When it comes to something cognitively demanding, we can only really pay attention to one thing at a time. This means that when it seems like we are doing different tasks, we are actually toggling between those tasks. To us, these transitions often feel seamless, which is why we think we are pulling it off, but we are just fooling ourselves because in reality we are

- **Going Slower**. David Meyer and Jeffrey Evans of the University of Michigan found that when you jump from one task to another, reorienting ourselves to the new set of rules for the new task takes time. If one is consistently multitasking, Meyer and Evans (American Psychological Association, 2006) found that tasks can take up to 40% longer!

- **Making More Mistakes**. Each time we jump between tasks we lose sight of the overall picture. When we return, we have to reorient to the larger picture, making the chance of making small mistakes much more likely (Willingham, 2010a).

- **Diminishing the Depth of Our Thinking**. Deep thought takes concentrated time, which means that if you don't stay put, your thinking will likely never leave the surface (Miller, 2016).

To paraphrase Dave Stuart Jr. (2018), who is a champion of saving teacher time: When responding to student work, just respond. When relaxing, relax. You will do a better of job of each and save a lot of time in the process.

The Last Word on Efficient Feedback

On the internet there exist any number of products and approaches that promise to cut your paper load by 75% instantly or allow you to read and respond to a paper in 5 minutes. These 5-minute solutions for a task as complex as reading and responding to student work generally work as well as 5-minute solutions for other complex problems, such as getting in shape or eating better, meaning they don't work over the long term—and can often do a great amount of harm in the process.

Nothing in this chapter will have you cutting your feedback time to next to nothing instantly. Responses to student writing are going to take time *if we do them right*—but our responses do not need to take all the time we currently pour into them. By employing these efficiency strategies, we can cut our time by 5% here and 10% there, and while those numbers don't seem dramatic, the average writing teacher, according to the study referenced earlier, spends roughly 360 hours a year responding to student papers. If true, this means each 5% increase in efficiency saves the average teacher 18 hours over the course of a year! Add up enough of such gains and the net result can quickly become whole weeks' worth of time that you can allocate to both your teaching and what are arguably the most important efficiency and effectiveness enhancers of all: predictable and regular time off, outside hobbies, sleep, and overall self-care.

Photo by Isabel Espinosa.

CHAPTER TWO

Giving More Effective Feedback
The Best Practices

The more I learned about feedback, the more I found the research to be maddeningly murky and contradictory in many areas. Consider praise, for example. The question of roughly how much of our feedback should be praise might seem pretty straightforward. Yet when I dug into the research, I read convincing arguments for praise being a deeply powerful tool (Cohen & Garcia, 2014), largely ineffective (Ryan, Miniis, & Koestner, 1983), very valuable in certain circumstances and very damaging in others (Gross-Loh, 2016), and not studied enough for us to have clear conclusions yet (Skipper & Douglas, 2012).

We look into praise more thoroughly in Chapter 4, but for now it serves as a good example of the type of discourse I found within the academic world concerning nearly every factor that goes into feedback. For academics, these nuanced debates and outcomes might be fine or even invigorating, but for the practicing teacher just looking to improve her practice, they can be overwhelming. I personally believe that the lack of clear or clearly articulated answers in so many areas concerning feedback is a large part of why so many ineffective feedback practices persist to the great detriment of our students. And according to John Hattie, ineffective feedback exists on a massive scale, with 32% of feedback having a negative effect—meaning it actually hurts student growth—and a large percentage of the effective feedback having a relatively small effect (Hattie & Timperley, 2007, p. 85).

Hattie is far from the only researcher to find such dire results concerning the average piece of feedback's efficacy, and based on those findings and what I've heard from many of the teachers I've met in recent years, it is fair to say that feedback is in the midst of a quiet and likely long-running effectiveness crisis. When one thinks of the millions of hours of feedback students get from teachers each year, such high levels of ineffective and minimally effective feedback lead to a scale of lost opportunities for students and lost hours for teachers that is both staggering and heartbreaking.

The aim of this chapter is to help reclaim some of those opportunities and hours by sifting through the noisy disagreements to find clear answers concerning which feedback practices lead to dramatic student improvement and which don't. Specifically, the chapter focuses around four key practices that enjoy wide support from both academics and teaching thought-leaders but remain relatively rare in actual practice. When implemented together, these keys can help teachers take fuller advantage of the hours spent on feedback by making it as effective as it can possibly be—and avoid common practices that waste our time and hurt our students.

Effectiveness Element #1: Feedback Should Be Provided by an Interested Reader, Not a Detached Authority

The question I am asked the most when I discuss feedback with teachers is, what are the maximum number of topics we should address when we give feedback? There are a lot of differing answers to this question out there. The *St. Martin's Sourcebook for Writing Tutors* by Christina Murphy (2018) recommends focusing on just two repeated higher order issues and one repeated mechanical mistake. Carol Jago (2005) suggests doing all the quick grammar and mechanical fixes but waiting to discuss content until a terminal note at the end. And in *Assessment for Learning*, Black, Harrison, Lee, Marshall, and William (2004) suggest that we only focus on one or maybe two features of the writing and ignore everything else. So who has the best approach? None of them, and also all of them.

I don't believe that there exists one golden number for the exact number of comments we should give to students. Any specific rule about what to respond to will inevitably work well for some students and not for others. For example, at the start of this year I read two students' narratives back-to-back. The first is titled "Melancholic Sentimentality," and it begins like this:

> Love is an equivocal and crippling beast that I do not wish to waste my time with. Attraction is fickle and fleeting. I claim these thoughts as my own, although I am not original in thinking them, because I have lived them and proven them to be true.

The second was simply titled "Personal Narrative," and it begins like this:

> "Get up" my mom called. I looked up at the clock it struck 6:30. "I don't wanna get up" I screamed. "Well you gotta catch your plane so get up". She said firmly. "ugghhh". I murmered. I got up my eyes widened as I looked around. All of my stuff was gone. I had forgot that I packed everything last night. I put my favorite pair of jeans on, then I put my favorite blue shirt and my blue jacket. I sprayed myself with my favorite clonge. "that smells good" I whispered.

It doesn't take a teacher to understand that these students have different styles, personalities, and understandings of writing. Any one rigid philosophy about the *right* number of comments would miss the mark for both kids. Instead, what we need to do is become an Interested Reader, which David Fuller (1987) defines as someone who

- Reads carefully
- Maintains a clear and specific role
- Remains aware of the context
- Stays sensitive to the student

In short, we need to think about the student, context, and our role as teacher, and then pay attention to the needs of the student. The difference between being an Interested Reader and what I refer to as the Detached Authority is nuanced but hugely important when it comes to feedback. While both the Interested Reader and Detached Authority respond to student writing by pointing out problem areas, offering suggestions, giving praise, and so on, a Detached Authority comes in with a preconceived set of rules and focuses on enforcing those; an Interested Reader focuses instead on the writer sitting in front of him and determining what will best help that writer grow. This distinction is commonly referred to as "teach the writer, not the writing," and while the difference between those two can appear subtle, the results are anything but. Figure 2.1 compares the two approaches.

A DETACHED AUTHORITY	AN INTERESTED READER
*Marks all moments where a preconceived set of rules are broken	*Marks only the issues that directly are connected to the lessons being learned in this paper
*Records all or most thoughts on the page while reading	*Records only the thoughts that connect to focus areas
*Largely communicates in curt shorthand	*Communicates in complete or nearly complete sentences and fully explains points that are made
*Uses the same approach and language for all students	*Adapts the approach and language to fit for the student

FIGURE 2.1 • Interested Reader and Detached Authority Comparison

For example, let's think about the two narrative snippets above. I know the student who wrote "Melancholic Sentimentality" read Oscar Wilde and Sylvia Plath between classes, and I could tell from a quick glance at her revision history that she had invested many, many hours into the piece already. For her, language is the most serious business, and if I let a hyphen take the spot of an em dash or allow a comma to continue on its merry way spliced, it would likely damage my credibility in her eyes.

When I responded to that first piece I thought about the student, context, and my role, and I decided to occupy a role that was closer to that of an editor than I normally would because I knew that was what the student was looking for. The little editorial details are also largely what she needs to progress forward. Of course, I was still strategic; I didn't mark every thought I had, but I also didn't shy away from technicalities and nuanced discussion of tone and grammar. Afterward this writer thanked me for the depth and care I showed.

As for "Personal Narrative," I knew the student came into my class with a dislike of writing, largely because he was embarrassed about his writing mechanics. At the same time, I knew from talking to him that he loved music and language (Drake being his favorite intersection of the two), and I'd seen him jotting down catchy rhymes in his notebook.

When I thought about the student, context, and my role, I knew that if I were to mark just the mechanical errors, there would be 15 different corrections by my count in the first five lines. At this point, the amount of ink, red or not, covering the page would likely send this student running for cover. So I decided instead to focus on just two topics: my appreciation of his word choice and the importance of complete sentences and punctuation. I hoped this approach would lower some of the walls he entered the classroom with and give him a bridge from which to access the information. I started with a comment discussing how both great song lyrics and great stories can be boiled down to word choice, detail, and rhythm, and his story was halfway there due to his thoughtful wording and details. This might have been an oversimplification, but it wasn't a lie. His repetition of *blue* when discussing his clothing, the whispered compliment he gives himself, the image of widening eyes—those are interesting word and detail choices, and my goal was to help him see that he was not as far away from strong writing as he thought he was. I then demonstrated the correct conventions of two things—commas and capitals—in the first few paragraphs of his piece and asked him to apply those lessons to the rest of the paper *while making sure he still maintains* his strong word choice.

Like the first student, this second student thanked me for my thoughtfulness, and more important, his final draft showed that he took my comments to heart, and it contained strikingly fewer conventional errors.

Effectiveness Element #2: Feedback Should Provide a Path Forward, Not an Autopsy

My search for better feedback practices began largely as a way to decrease the weight papers put on my life. Consequently, the first time I came across the idea that we should give students feedback as they draft their work (in what is commonly called the *formative stage*), instead of just at the end (or what is commonly called the *summative stage*), I laughed out loud.

Reading, responding to, and assessing my students' papers once had already pushed me to a breaking point. How could I possibly double my workload by adding an additional round of reading and responding to papers somewhere in the middle? Clearly this suggestion was one of those ideas from academia that looked good on paper but was simply too much work in actual practice.

However, the topic of giving robust formative feedback continued to come up repeatedly as I dug deeper into feedback best practices. Every major published writing teacher throughout the last 30 years—including, but definitely not limited to, Nancy Atwell, Kelly Gallagher, Linda Rief, Penny Kittle, Jim Burke, Donald Murray, and Linda Christensen—argues for it. It is also advocated by the National Writing Project (NWP), the National Council of Teachers of English (NCTE), and the International Literacy Association (ILA). Scores of academic studies and literature reviews have made compelling cases that shifting the bulk of our feedback to formative stages can potentially double the speed of student learning, dramatically speed up the learning of ELL (English language learner) students, and significantly shrink the size of the multiple common achievement gaps (Ferris, 1995; Fisher & Frey, 2013; Volante & Beckett, 2011).

As I continued to encounter this idea of formative feedback time and again, I had to admit that it made a lot of sense. When students do a final draft, the very name implies that it is time to move on—and students tend to be both busy and strategic. They have five or six other classes, a lot of assignments, and plenty vying for their attention. When looking at it from the perspective of managing a heavy workload or trying to keep up a specific GPA, if they have already received or lost the points they were going to get or lose, moving quickly through the feedback and then moving on often appear to even the most committed students to be sensible moves.

Students also regularly get so embarrassed by their errors on final drafts that they resist seriously revisiting them. Every year I have dozens of students who try at some point to turn in *final* drafts that are largely unchanged versions of previous drafts. I used to get upset with these students, but now my policy is to hold short conferences with them where we get to the bottom of why they won't do a revision. The students' initial responses tend to be all over the place, ranging from braggadocious (*I don't really need to revise*) to unsure (*I don't know how to change my writing*), but as the conversations go deeper, nearly all boil down to one element: Students don't want to take a close look at their own work because they are embarrassed by it in some way.

In his book *Embarrassment: And the Emotional Underlife of Learning*, Thomas Newkirk (2017) explains that this kind of embarrassment runs rampant throughout our schools because of the intersection of two well-documented behaviors: the spotlight effect, which is the common belief that others pay way more attention to us than they actually do, and the loss aversion, which prioritizes the avoidance of risk over grabbing opportunities because, according to Nobel Laureate Daniel Kahneman (2011), "organisms that treat threats as more urgent than opportunities have a better chance to survive and reproduce" (p. 282). Compound these two behaviors with the insecurities of adolescence and the uncertain nature of writing, and it is clear why so many students look for the nearest recycling bin as soon as they receive final draft feedback.

Eventually, after hearing enough arguments for it, I gave formative feedback a chance and I haven't looked back since. Few, if any, changes I've made in my teaching have made as rapid and as positive an impact. This is largely because the very things that lead to many students ignoring summative feedback—loss aversion, spotlight effects, and taking a strategic, pragmatic approach to school—all push students to actually read and think through feedback if it is given in formative stages. If the teacher has provided the student with a roadmap to a better paper and will be paying close attention, the biggest risk for students is often to do nothing or instantly recycle that roadmap.

Also, I came to learn that formative feedback doesn't have to double the time we spend with papers. In fact, there are a number of practices that can allow us to provide powerful formative feedback without taking home a single paper. Here are some of the most effective.

ASSESSING PREWRITING

Students often don't like prewriting. For many, prewriting seems like another unnecessary hoop to jump through in school, and so they avoid it or do just enough not to lose points. When those things happen though, both the students and their teachers end up missing out on a golden opportunity.

For students, prewriting gives a space to sort their ideas out before entering the pressure cooker of writing a paper, which often leads to better papers in less time. Planes that are built while flying generally can't fly very fast or straight, after all. For teachers, student prewriting provides a wonderful opportunity to give meaningful formative feedback in almost no time at all. When we ask students to share their research or the narrative arc of an upcoming story before they write it, we can assess those major elements and offer real feedback in mere seconds—seconds that could save minutes for teachers and hours for students down the road!

Figures 2.2 and 2.3 show two examples of prewriting that can be assessed and turned into useful feedback in seconds. Figure 2.2 shows a student-drawn map of the setting of his personal narrative. Having students draw detailed, descriptive maps before writing a story or narrative is a common technique to help students generate and visualize those little details that bring stories alive, but these maps also provide visual outlines that teachers can, at a glance, assess for everything from characterization to story structure.

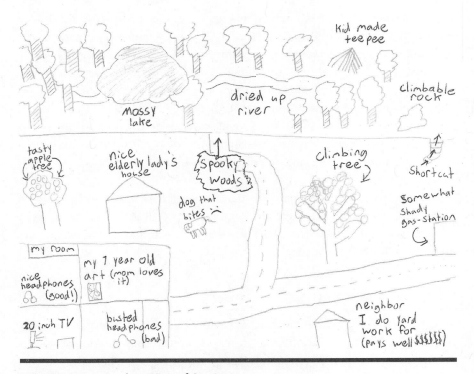

FIGURE 2.2 • Student Map of Setting

Figure 2.3 is an outline I use for research papers. It is structured like a narrative story arc because I find having students think about research papers as stories helps them avoid two of the most common research paper issues: disorganized papers that read like lists of information and bland, uninteresting prose. At the same time, the narrative structure of the outline also allows the teacher to tell at a quick glance which students are the most at risk to falling into dull or poorly organized papers, allowing her to allocate her attention accordingly.

Your Topic: Frogs

Your Central Idea/Question/Problem:

Frogs matter more than we know, and they are in danger.

Your Hook Idea:

Our planet is littered with animals of all shapes and sizes. From the mighty bison that once ruled the planes of America to the towering blue whales of the oceans. I, however, would like to focus on the in between. Those amphibious creatures that spend part of their life in the water and part on the land. The frogs.

The Rising Action (The Key Topics in the Order That They Will Build):

1. Frog basics

2. The threats facing frogs, especially the chytrid fungus

3. Without action, frogs may disappear altogether

4. This would deprive the world of amazing frogs like the Vietnamese Mossy Frog, Glass Frog, and Venezuelan Pebble Toad

5. It would severely damage ecosystems

6. It would hurt humans

Climax (Where You Resolve/Discuss the Central Idea/Question/Problem):

We can do something! There is no cure for chytrid fungus, but we do have the ability to implement interventions to stop the spread and increase habitat to act as a firewall.

Resolution (Where You "Tie Up Loose Ends" or Look to the Future):

A vision of a world full of a beautiful array of frogs!

FIGURE 2.3 • Research Paper Outline

GIVING WHOLE-CLASS FEEDBACK IN EARLY STAGES

In the earliest stages of papers, it doesn't make a lot of sense to spend hours digging through the rough clay of student drafts with a fine-tooth comb. Instead, it makes a lot more sense to give whole-class feedback, which is an idea that goes back a long way. In fact, the first instance I can find is in a 1962 *English Journal* article in which Eric Johnson reported that he collected and read early stages of polished papers until he found the most common issues. Then he'd build the next day's lesson around those issues.

I have no doubt that this idea goes back further, but I have seen it echoed recently by Kelly Gallagher (2006), Allison Marchetti and Rebekah O'Dell (2015), and Dave Stuart Jr. (2018), among others. Although whole-class feedback is not as personalized as individual feedback, it allows us to provide solid feedback to students fast. I have found that I can generally identify common errors in a stack of papers with surprising accuracy in 10 to 15 minutes.

When we use whole class feedback, we often don't even need to collect the papers. We can circulate and jot down notes about the most common issues as the students draft and then take some of the time saved by not reading through all the papers to craft a meaningful lesson, full of mentor texts and clear action steps, for *the next day.*

USING MICRO-CONFERENCES

Conferences are one of the fastest accelerators of student growth that we have. Even short snippets of conversation can lead to remarkable learning. Conferences can be logistically tricky though. Take my American Literature classes, for example, both of which currently sit at 34 students. If I have a 5-minute conference with each student and factor in a minute of transition time, the amount of time needed comes to 210 minutes, which is 82% of the time I have with students each week. Add in little details like taking roll, providing directions, logging into and off of computers, and so on, and 5-minute conferences with each student require nearly an entire week of class time.

While investing large chunks of time into conferences is indeed worthwhile (Chapter 3 discusses the essential role conferences play in the writing classroom and how to hold full-length conferences as fast as possible), for most of us, there simply aren't the weeks in the school year to do multiple larger conferences in each unit. Instead, we can use what I call micro-conferences, which are more tightly focused conversations designed to take a minute or less. If structured right, micro-conferences take place in even the biggest classes within the confines of one class period, often with time to spare.

While the exact structures of micro-conferences vary according to the topic and situation, they tend to work best with some of the same basic components:

1. The teacher identifies one or two focus areas for the students and provides a mentor text or short activity to demonstrate to the students what she is looking for.

2. Students engage in some sort of self-assessment activity where they assess their current understanding and performance concerning the focus area(s).

3. Once a student completes the self-assessment, she signals for the teacher to come over, which begins the conference. (If the teacher isn't available to conference right away, the student can use her initial self-assessment to improve the draft until the teacher is available.)

4. Each micro-conference starts with the student telling the teacher about his self-assessment and what he noticed. It is important to start conferences with the student talking first because the student has already prepared, making him better prepared to jump right in.

5. The teacher then gives her thoughts and the conversation continues as needed. Sometimes the conversations are barely more than 10 or 15 seconds because the student clearly understands the focus area and what she needs to do; other times they will go for a couple minutes because the student has misconceptions or doesn't fully understand something. The goal should be to keep even the longest micro-conferences to 1 to 2 minutes maximum though.

6. If the conference will need more than a few minutes to conclude or seems to be expanding into wider topics, the teacher can give the student some sort of tangible task for the moment and politely ask to stop back by in a few minutes once everyone else has had a micro-conference (or determine a time outside of class to discuss it further). This response acknowledges the student's needs while also making sure that everyone will get a chance to talk to the teacher.

Let's consider an example of a micro-conference from a recent class. At the time, I noticed that students were struggling with paraphrasing, using direct quotes, and blending research in the research papers we were writing. These are tricky topics, so I decided to do a micro-conference that looked like this:

It began with a mentor text, a student paper from the previous year that did a good job of paraphrasing and generally blending the student's ideas and voice with the ideas and voices from the research. As a class we read the paper and highlighted the paraphrased sections and underlined the direct quotes. We then discussed afterward why the mentor text worked regarding its use of paraphrased and quoted research.

Next, the students picked a page of their papers and highlighted their paraphrased sections and underlined their direct quotes. They had to reflect on the following questions:

- Do you think you have too much or too little paraphrasing? Too many or too few direct quotes?
- Do all your moments of paraphrasing seem like you truly put them into your own words?
- On a scale of 1 to 10, how well do you think you blended your voice and ideas with the voices and ideas from the research you used? What could you do to get a 10?

By the times students called me over, the combination of the visually distinctive coding of the paraphrased and quoted sections combined with their reflective questions and self-ranking allowed us to almost instantly jump into substantive conversation that could almost as quickly lead to equally substantive suggestions and ideas about where to go from there.

This chapter discusses best practices for giving formative feedback to an entire larger essay later, but it is essential that we don't forget these other smaller formative assessment practices.

They are like the neutron stars of the writing classroom; the space they take up is tiny, but they are heavy with meaningful lessons. They provide a path forward for students because we give meaningful feedback, participate in ongoing collaboration instead of intermittent judgment, and increase moments of meaningful interaction, which has been shown to make students more engaged and more resilient (Desautels, 2018). And perhaps most important, they do it all without us having to add a lot more to our grading loads or even take a single extra paper home.

Effectiveness Element #3: Most Feedback Should Be Focused on Actions, Not Reactions

Smaller-scale formative feedback via prewriting assessment, whole-class teaches, and micro-conferences can have sizable impact, but eventually students reach a point where they need larger, personalized, and more global feedback. This is what I call *comprehensive feedback*, and it is where the teacher reads and responds to a piece of larger, polished writing in its totality.

Comprehensive feedback is generally the most time-consuming feedback that teachers give. In my early years of teaching, it would take me an average of 20 minutes to give comprehensive feedback to each two-to-three-page polished student paper that came across my desk, a rate that equates to roughly 53 hours needed for me to give feedback to the 159 young minds entrusted to me this semester for *each* paper assigned.

Now I can read and respond to similar papers in an average of 8 to 10 minutes by following the practices outlined in the first chapter: staying in the right mind-set, going digital, having some automation, and of course avoiding the urge to mark everything. And while that is a huge improvement, it is still a massive time commitment, totaling over 23 hours to give a comprehensive response to each student for each paper assigned. Considering the time investment required to do that, I want to make sure that my comments have a large enough impact to warrant the hours put into them, and when one looks at the research, there is one factor that usually seems to separate effective comprehensive feedback from ineffective comprehensive feedback: whether it is focused on actions or reactions.

THE PROBLEM OF REACTIVE FEEDBACK

A common misconception about feedback is that it is our reaction to a piece of writing. Feedback is related to our reaction, which is our initial response to something, but good feedback is generally not our unfiltered reaction. To understand why, let's look at reactions and feedback from the perspective of a track coach, a role I served for a number of years.

The hardest race in track according to most runners is the 800-meter race because it lives in the strange area between sprints and distance events. One cannot sprint 800 meters, but one can't jog it either. Instead, one must do an odd blend of the two, and its difficulty means that new 800-meter runners stumble their way into plenty of teachable moments. One common problem occurs when a runner sprints too fast at the start of the race and burns out their muscles. This causes them to, in track speak, "hit the wall": The muscles give out in such a dramatic fashion that it quite literally looks like the runner has slammed into an invisible wall. My internal reaction as a coach when watching a runner hit the wall for the first time often went something like this:

> *Slow down . . . Slow down . . . Oh no, that looks like way too fast of a start! This is either going to be a record or end badly, probably the latter . . . Yeah, she is hitting the wall . . . Poor kid . . . Important lesson, but that stinks . . . The rest of the race is not going to be fun. Please just finish . . .*

In this you see my unedited second-by-second reactive response to what I'm observing. It is blunt (*Poor kid. Important lesson, but that stinks*), emotional (*Oh no, that looks like way too fast of a start!*), not super constructive (*The rest of the race is not going to be fun*), and doesn't look to the future at all.

That is not at all what my feedback to the young runner would be after she crosses the finish line, however. Instead, my feedback would be something like this:

> *I love that you went for it. But the first 200 meters of your race was 29 seconds. That is a 1:56 pace, which would put you within a second of the all-time American women's record; I don't think we are quite there yet. By contrast your last 200 meters was almost 50 seconds, which is far slower than any section should be from you. Next time, let's try to have more even times for each 200 meters, because that is the way to maximize your energy. Let's start by having you go out in 38 seconds and see if you can maintain that pace the whole time. We can practice that pace in practice next week to help you get used to it.*

In this you see something very different than my reaction. My feedback is positive and personable (*I love that you went for it*), gives context (*. . . would put you within a second of the American record; I don't think we are quite there yet . . .*), sets up specific goals for the future (*Let's try to have more even 200-meter splits, as that is the way to maximize your energy*), and give steps she can take toward those goals (*Let's start by having you go out in 38 seconds. We can practice that pace in practice next week so you get used to it*).

In most situations in our lives we don't give our reaction as our feedback. When we are sitting at a staff meeting and hear a colleague say something we disagree with, we don't shout out, "That idea is ridiculous!" even if we initially feel it.

Instead, we translate our reaction into something more useful. The same thing is true with our friends, partners, and children. It even is true with our students in most contexts—unless we are giving them feedback on their writing, where putting blunt and rather unfiltered reactions is strangely the norm.

Remember that example from Chapter 1 of how I used to respond to student work (see Figure 1.5)? That was a reaction-heavy approach to feedback. My comments on that paper are essentially a running list of my reactions set in amber between the margins and lines. If we want our feedback to be as effective as possible, one key thing we need to do is to reverse this norm of treating reactions as feedback and shift our feedback to being more focused on actions. This makes our feedback far more likely to be received and internalized, and it also allows us to give feedback in less time, because focusing on actions frees us from a number of common time-consuming and yet largely ineffective practices.

When it comes to making this shift, there are three key practices that can help keep us focused on actions, not reactions. They are using the Describe-Evaluate-Success Model, providing a path so students can do the work for themselves, and identifying and focusing on core growth goals.

THE DESCRIBE-EVALUATE-SUCCESS MODEL

If a student has a voice that doesn't quite work for a piece of writing, a common approach would be to give the student some feedback like this:

> *"Your voice in this doesn't work. Make sure your voice fits for your audience and purpose."*

On the surface this might seem fine, but there are two major problems with this response. The first is that there is a high likelihood that it will be misunderstood by the student. Studies have found almost 50% of teacher feedback, including many comments that seem incredibly obvious to teachers, might be misconstrued by the students (Chanock, 2000). I've found that such common teacher words as *voice, flow, analysis,* and *clarity*—are so broad that students easily misunderstand what we are saying when we use them.

The other issue is that it leads with judgment, and humans are highly defensive creatures. For many of our students, even the slightest perceived judgments can often set off a defensive response that essentially causes them to block out much of the feedback that comes next. For many of them, starting by stating that something doesn't work will likely be enough to do that.

In a world where 50% of comments are potentially misunderstood and student defensiveness is set on a hair trigger, taking an approach called Describe-Evaluate-Success with feedback offers protection against both issues. The concept behind Describe-Evaluate-Success is that we should start each piece of feedback with a brief, neutral description of what we noticed, then we move into some form of evaluation of what we observed, and we end with providing steps the student can take toward success (Hart-Davidson, 2014). In the case of the comment on voice, it might look something like this actual comment I gave a student last year:

> *I notice that most of the paper is written in an academic tone and then you refer to Kate Chopin as "a badass" in the conclusion. This statement, while funny and maybe true, wasn't consistent with the voice of the rest of the paper and served as more of a distraction than a strong ending. In your revision, is there a way you can get across what an amazingly strong person Chopin was while keeping you tone consistent?*

On the surface, both this comment and one before discuss voice, but that is where the similarities end. While the first comment could easily be misconstrued (*what does he mean by voice? Is it my sentence structure, word choice, ideas?*), having to describe the issue first forced me to get to the root of the issue, which was her word choice and tone. Further, by starting with what is written on the page instead of starting with my judgment of her choices, the odds are far better that the student won't feel as judged, making her more open to the feedback. In fact, when I shared the comment above with the student, she laughed out loud at the fact that she called Kate Chopin a "badass" and said, "Yeah, maybe not the right word," with a giant smile on her face. Further, the impact of the comment was apparent when her new revised conclusion had replaced "badass" by referring to Chopin as "unique," "recognizable," and capable of creating "female characters of varying, but never mono-layered, complexity and depth." Figure 2.4 shows some examples of how to rephrase common teacher comments using the Describe-Evaluate-Success Model.

STUDENTS DO THE WORK

In recent years, the term *feedforward*, often first attributed to Marshall Goldsmith (Hirsch, 2017), has become increasingly popular. At its core, feedforward is just the idea that feedback should connect the present state with the future goals in clearly defined steps. This is strikingly similar to what John Hattie has been

COMMON TEACHER COMMENTS	DESCRIBE-EVALUATE-SUCCESS VERSION
"Your topic sentences don't work. Make sure they set up the topics of the paragraphs and the paragraphs stay focused on those topics the entire time."	"I notice that this topic sentence talks about how homework can contribute to student stress, but most of the paragraph talks about how students don't get enough sleep. This drifting of topics throughout a paragraph is something I've also seen in other paragraphs. Readers generally look to the first line of a paragraph for the topic, so I would like you to go through and make sure the topic at the start and end of each paragraph are the same."
"Your wording in this could be stronger. Try to incorporate more vivid and interesting words."	"In this climactic scene you refer to yourself as scared, happy, and excited. These words are a bit broad and really common, meaning that we don't get a full sense of how you feel in that key moment. Try replacing these with words that are more specific and unique that can better express how you felt."
"Your flow in this paper is choppier than I'd like. Work on improving your sentence structure to make it flow better."	"The vast majority of your sentences are shorter than ten words. This gives your writing a choppy feel at times. A way to improve your flow would be to have more sentence length variation. I suggest getting this by combining some sentences and adding more details to others."

FIGURE 2.4 • Describe-Evaluate-Success Model

saying for decades, with his most recent work on feedback, *Visible Learning Feedback* (Hattie & Clarke, 2018), defining feedback as "information about the task that fills a gap between what is understood and what is aimed to be understood" (p. 3).

Both Goldsmith and Hattie emphasize that feedback is about providing a path. It is not about walking the path for the students by fixing their errors. While we want to give them a clear explanation of what is happening in it and offer steps that can be taken to get there, when we jump in and correct things for our students, we are the ones doing the work, not them. In these moments, we are forgetting that struggle is a necessary component of learning. If students don't have to figure out the answers for themselves, they won't remember very much because they haven't had to work for it. This is a point that Daniel Coyle (2009) makes in his book *The Talent Code* by giving the reader a list of related word pairs and asking them to look at it for a few seconds, turn the page, and try to remember as many as possible (pp. 16–17). I've recreated such a list with new words in Figure 2.5 to demonstrate.

A	B
sunrise/sunset	ice/cr_am
peanut butter/jelly	table/ch_irs
sun/stars	f_st/forward
movie/popcorn	pepperoni/p_zza
snow/ice	c_ffee/tea
car/keys	y_sterday/today
apples/oranges	light/h_use
country/city	t_xt/call
chocolate/chip	rain/cl_ud
knife/fork	s_n/moon

FIGURE 2.5 • Example of Coyle's Word List

How will my students know the right answers if I don't show them?

If it feels like a student needs an example of how to fix a repeated error (e.g., a comma splice or an unclear topic sentence), I will make one correction and take the time to explain what I did and why. But after that, I will state that I expect *the student* to go through and use that model to eliminate the issue throughout her paper. If I think this will still be too complex a task, I will sometimes also highlight lines where that same issue appears, so the student has some further direction concerning where the issues lie.

According to Coyle, the average person remembers 300% more words from Column B than from Column A despite the fact that the pairings are otherwise similar. The reason? We have to work for a brief second to understand the second column because of the missing letter, and that small moment of struggle is enough to make the list exponentially more memorable.

Once students know that we won't make the changes for them yet we expect them to revise, they will be far more likely to put in the effort needed to get it there, which in turn will make it far more likely they will learn the lesson. Further, doing this is also good practice from an efficiency standpoint. It takes way less time to offer destinations and potential steps than it takes to troubleshoot problematic sentences, cross out redundancies, organize a paper, and otherwise solve all the problems for the students!

CORE GROWTH AREAS

The first chapter discusses how not over-commenting on a paper is a win from both efficiency and effectiveness standpoints because it frees up time for us to fully teach the lessons we do cover without adding more time to our responding of papers. This approach only works, though, when the students also use that extra space to fully learn the lessons we want them to focus on.

This is why I identify one or two core growth areas in a short note that I write at the top of the student's paper to frame how I want them to read the comments in the paper itself. This note is meant to shine a spotlight on the areas of the greatest concern in an effort to nudge students to take the time to seriously grapple with and move forward in those areas during the revision process.

The other advantage of clearly identifying core growth goals is that students can easily misunderstand what they should focus on in a revision. To us, the scale of importance of each comment we give—whether it is a major issue or a little side note—is likely clear, but the same might not be said for students. Putting these goals at the top guards against this by giving students a roadmap with which to read our feedback.

To further brighten that spotlight, I include a special category on the final rubric labeled "Mr. Johnson's Growth Areas" that is worth significant points, allocated on the basis of how much the students grappled with and improved in those core areas. Figure 2.6 shows that category in one of my final rubrics. (Reading note: Across Chapters 2 and 3, I revisit this rubric multiple times to break down why I use rubrics for final drafts of polished papers and to show you how each category develops and is used.)

CATEGORY	CRITERIA	POINTS POSSIBLE
Make Me Care	— It has uncertainty and serious stakes that create tension. — It contains a lot of specific details and imagery. — It uses almost all indirect characterization. — The words are carefully chosen and emotional. — You feel like you know the author; it has minimal cliché usage.	__/20
Story Arc	— The setting grabs the reader and makes a promise that this will be worth his/her/their time; it contains interesting questions. — There is a clear problem that builds to a climax; the climax has tension and is some of your best writing. — The resolution ties up all the loose ends; if no resolution is present, there is a good reason for it.	__/10

(Continued)

(Continued)

CATEGORY	CRITERIA	POINTS POSSIBLE
Grammar	– All commas are used correctly. – There is interesting use of advanced grammatical techniques to enhance the piece. – There are no nonpurposeful run-ons and fragments. – The grammar is polished according to Standard English conventions (or has good reasons for why it doesn't follow the conventions).	__/10
Mr. Johnson's Growth Areas	You spend time grappling with Mr. Johnson's core growth areas; you move forward in those areas in significant ways. Mr. Johnson's core growth areas for me include (1) (2) (3)	__/15
Your Goals	You put serious effort toward improving in your goal areas. Your personal goals are (1) (2) (3)	__/15
The Rest	– It is well organized and has no sudden transitions. – It has interesting language and a clear and consistent voice. – The topic is compelling and interesting. – The writing in the paper works because . . .	__/30
Total	Comments:	__/100

FIGURE 2.6 • Personal Essay Rubric, With Focus on Growth Areas

Effectiveness Element #4: Feedback and Assessment Should Be Separated

Earlier in this chapter, I mentioned that it used to take me 20 minutes to read and respond to a student paper. That response included comments on the paper itself, a filled-out rubric, and a grade. Now, I read and respond to each polished paper twice—once to give formative feedback and once again at the end—and I do both in a combined time of less than 15 minutes on average. I also see my students understanding and internalizing my feedback at rates I would have thought unimaginable when I first began my study of feedback.

So how is it possible that I can read and respond to a paper twice in less than 75% of time it used to take me to read and respond to it once *while also getting a far better result*? The key, beyond being choosy about what I comment on, is I don't put written feedback on final drafts.

When I tell teachers this, the look I often get is one of *"ah, so that is where you cut the corner to save time."* And on the surface, this practice may look and feel like a corner being cut. But when we dig into it, there is actually a lot of evidence to support the idea that feedback and assessment should be separated. Although providing feedback and assessing a paper (more commonly referred to as *grading a paper*) are often used interchangeably as synonyms, they are actually very different activities. Feedback is about showing students how to rise to the next level by illuminating paths forward. Grading is about rating a student's current skills and relaying that information to anyone interested.

When we do these two competing activities simultaneously, one is bound to get less attention, and it is generally our feedback—the feedback we poured dozens of hours into—that gets ignored for the following reasons:

- When a grade is present, student attention and mental energy tends to focus on the grade, limiting the attention and energy paid to other feedback present (Belanger & Allingham, 2004).

- The grade can serve as an indicator to many students that an assignment and the associated learning are done, further limiting the amount of attention and energy given to the written feedback. (Belanger & Allingham, 2004)

- When students are ashamed by a low grade, they often avoid the feedback as a defense against further embarrassment. (Newkirk, 2017)

- When students are surprised by an unexpectedly high grade, they tend to bask in the grade while growing disinterested in further growth because they have already achieved more than they expected. (Belanger & Allingham, 2004)

- A constant stream of either low or high grades can reinforce a fixed mindset in students that they are *good* or *bad* writers. Either one of these can slow writing growth because the *good* writers will often feel they can let their foot off the gas while the *bad* writers often feel that it isn't even worth the effort.

By focusing one read on feedback and the other on assessment, we avoid these pitfalls and maximize the effectiveness of both our feedback and assessment. Further, we can go a lot faster because each reading is focused on one task, making 15 minutes or less to respond reasonable because we only do feedback and assessment one time each.

Isn't 5 to 6 minutes too fast to read and grade a final paper?

Five or six minutes for a paper is fast, but I have an incredibly effective technological aide: revision and comment history. Pretty much any modern word processing program has a full history of revisions and comments. Google even has a button that pops up when someone else has made edits to a piece called "See new changes" that highlights exactly what changes have been made since we last looked at a piece. Here is what it looks like:

> Growing up, my family's garage was bigger than some of my friend's houses. We would travel to enchanting parts of the world all reasonably to wealthy areas in Europe. And then there was Cuba- thought- provoking Cuba. The painstaking heat shocked me, but- the intense poverty shocked me more. A little girl about aroundthe age of 7seven years old came up to me. Her clothes torn. Her desperate eyes looked at me before she put out her dry unwashed hands. I pulled out I gave a her a few bills gave them to her before she rushed back to her younger brother. Being around a different world of people changed my thoughts and made me a more caring person.After experiencing this I have donated more to the less fortunate people who are struggling.

> We visited a neighborhood youth school and a group of children waved me over. ~~I was~~ ~~around other children and worked with them.~~ Although I am not fluent in Spanish, my 4 years of experience helped me to communicate. ~~Words were not my main use of connection. Passion~~

These tools allow us to quickly re-enter the world of the paper and assess/grade it using our previous read as a foundation that allows us to assess it much faster than if it were an entirely new piece. By using them and not using comments, 5 to 6 minutes to read and evaluate a summative draft suddenly seems quite reasonable.

THE ROLE OF CO-CONSTRUCTED RUBRICS

It should be noted that just because we don't write comments on a final draft doesn't mean that students can't learn from it. Rubrics, while dangerous if poorly designed (see Chapter 1), can be a powerful, fast feedback tool for final drafts if carefully designed and—this the key part—co-constructed with students.

The first time I saw a rubric co-constructed by teachers and their students was in Kelly Gallagher's (2006) *Teaching Adolescent Writers*, and the idea was a revelation for me. Traditionally, determining the criteria for success on a paper and design- ing the rubric have been the undisputed realms of the teacher. We are the ones who have studied in college both our content and how humans learn, can recite in our sleep the various district and state standards, and have extensive experi- ence assessing student work. For many of us, we have more years of experience than our students have years of life, but if we want our students to learn from our assessment and rubrics, inviting the students to have a say is incredibly effective.

Before moving on, I want to make it clear that having students co-construct criteria does not mean that they get to determine how we assess or grade their papers. It also does not mean watering down our standards or that students get to choose to study whenever they want. As teachers, we bring great knowledge concerning what makes writing and student writers work, and it is essential that this knowledge still lie at the heart of decision making in the classroom.

Instead, when we co-construct criteria, we invite students to think closely about the standards and topics covered in class and what they mean for the student's writing. That close thought concerning the categories is what allows a rubric to be a meaningful source of feedback instead of a series of boxes that need to be checked off because students have a deeper understanding of what it means.

On the surface, standards and rubrics may seem like rather dull topics from a student perspective, but I find that if structured right and done earnestly, students greatly enjoy these moments of co-construction. They also really appreciate them because they walk away with a view behind the curtain and a deeper understanding of how both the classroom and our assessment of writing really works.

Generally, co-constructing criteria works best if it takes place somewhere in the middle of the writing process, usually when students have a full draft of their paper but the final draft still looms a fair distance on the horizon. I used to do this at the start of the unit, but I discovered that students do a better job of talking about criteria after they have seen a number of examples, had some lessons on craft, and done some initial writing.

To begin the co-constructing process, I hand out a blank rubric with my core criteria listed. The core criteria in my rubric are the focus areas of the unit, and they are drawn from a range of places: observations I've made about student writing during previous papers or in the initial drafting phases, standards that are required by the state and/or district, or other traits I know as essential for the genre we are working on. Wherever they come from, it's helpful to focus on no more than three, because any more than that can overwhelm students.

Take another look at Figure 2.6. The three core criteria—Make Me Care, Story Arc, and Grammar—align with my district's standards, and I've found them to be critical regarding whether a personal essay succeeds or fails. It's important, though, that my students understand the criteria for each of these areas, so we co-construct the criteria by studying curated segments of mentor texts that show the core criteria in practice. Some of these are segments of student and/or professional texts we've already read and some are new. Some are good, some are great, and, depending on the situation, some might have some issues. Whatever these mentor texts are, they generally have been chosen to seed debate about what the core criteria mean and what the expectations for each criteria should be.

For an example, let's take the first criteria listed for my narrative, Make Me Care, which comes from a TED Talk by screenwriter Andrew Stanton (2012) on the keys to telling a good story. Stanton claims that making the audience care is the core storytelling commandment. He says that it doesn't matter whether we emotionally care, intellectually care, or aesthetically care, so long as we care. Everything else about storytelling is secondary to that. I've found this indeed true when it comes to personal essays and that "make me care" is a wonderful explanation of what a great many devices ranging from imagery to indirect characterization are meant to accomplish.

Last year, to seed our creation of the rubric, I gave students the following mentor texts—student college admission essays from previous years—that made both me and the admissions officers care.

EXAMPLE #1

These days I think back to what my parents must have felt. Checking on their six year old only to find the indent of where he once was. Seeing the trail of things bumped over as I tiptoed out in the darkness and fearing the worst for their child's well-being. However I was fine, sitting on the beach feeling the sand between my toes and looking up into the heavens. There was something beautiful about the clusters of sparkling stars that filled the black canvas of the sky. I had a compulsion. I would lie awake night after night unable to sleep until I could get glimpse of the night sky. I wanted to discover what our universe was hiding. So night after night I would sneak down to the beach of our cabin. I knew there was something waiting for me, for us, up there.

EXAMPLE #2

Peeking between each of my fingers, I saw her alternating pink and purple polished nails, and that put my mouth in my stomach. Those little plastic blobs of paint and glitter that never quite stayed in their rightful boundaries reminded me that she was still a little girl, pigtails and polish and all. She was just a little girl trying to hold on to her youth.

More than the doctors, more than the parents and friends, I knew that feeling of watching your childhood slip away, piece by piece. Little by little. It was the touch of the cool squeaky school gym floor that nestled the weight of my body—off to the sidelines—because according to the doctors "dodgeball was bad," and so was soccer, and dancing, and basketball. It was the sight of the balls flying above, one by one, and knowing every single colored dreamy whirr was out of reach. I still had my hands outstretched though because I was just a little girl trying to hold on to my youth.

After reading these, the students briefly discussed the traits that go into making a reader care. They talked about word choice, expectations, use of literary devices, voice, and emotion. During this time, I played the role of secretarial gadfly, asking questions, pushing students to go further, reminding them of previous lessons from class on these subjects, and filling in the blank Make Me Care section of the rubric under a document camera. While there is nothing wrong with the teacher adding a thought or two during this process, the main goal of this is to get the students thinking through what the rubric means; so that is the bulk of what we do. I've learned the hard way that if students get the sense that what the teacher is really doing is a "lecto-scussion," or a discussion that is less about exploring ideas and more about guessing at what the teacher wants to say, many students will instantly turn their attention off, because their input at that point is not really needed. Further, when we engage in mandates masquerading as collaboration, the effect is often that the students feel less valued and involved, not more.

We followed the same protocol for Story Arc and Grammar. At the end of the discussion, the first three rows of the rubric looked like what's shown in Figure 2.7. (This full rubric is available on the companion website at **resources .corwin.com/flashfeedback** along with rubrics created for other common genres of writing: narrative, analytical essay, research paper.)

Once the teacher goes through all the criteria, the final step in classes with grades is for students to debate how many points each category should be worth. To do this, give a set number of points for the three sections—it was 40 of the 100 total points for the personal essay above—and students make arguments for how to allocate those points that are grounded in the mentor texts. The teacher's role is to take notes, ask questions, and keep score.

For many teachers, giving the students a say in the point values might seem like giving too much power to the students, but I would argue that the risk is quite low and the reward quite high. The students only argue about a fraction of the points and the ultimate decision for point distribution remains the teacher's. Yet for students, having a say in the grade is a powerful attention-generating device, and it gets them seriously weighing what they should prioritize while writing. Whenever we do this part, my students almost universally lean forward on the very fronts of their chairs, and the debate about relative value often pushes their understanding of the concepts and rubric to a whole new level.

CATEGORY	CRITERIA	POINTS POSSIBLE
Make Me Care	– It has uncertainty and serious stakes that create tension. – It contains a lot of specific details and imagery. – It uses almost all indirect characterization. – The words are carefully chosen and emotional. – You feel like you know the author; it has minimal cliché usage.	__/20
Story Arc	– The setting grabs the reader and makes a promise that this will be worth his/her/their time; it contains interesting questions. – You have a clear problem that builds to a climax; the climax has tension and is some of your best writing. – The resolution ties up all the loose ends; if no resolution is present, there is a good reason for it.	__/10
Grammar	– Your commas are used right. – You use advanced grammatical techniques to enhance your piece. – You have no nonpurposeful run-ons and fragments. – The grammar is polished according to Standard English conventions (or has good reasons where it doesn't follow the conventions).	__/10

FIGURE 2.7 • Co-Constructed Criteria for Personal Essays

The building of this rubric is meant in part to help students better understand the writing process, the key criteria of the genre we are writing in, and writing in general. But its main advantage, from both time-saving and effectiveness perspectives, is that it allows a teacher to put minimal or even no written feedback on students' final drafts and still pass along important messages because the students understand the rubric so well.

Since I began co-creating rubrics, I have felt released from the need to comment or write notes to the vast majority of students because I feel they know why they got the score they received. This saves me time that I can reallocate to formative feedback where it will have the biggest impact. Of course, I do still write some short notes on some summative drafts, but it is only when I sense a misunderstanding the rubric won't fix or there is a pressing point it won't make. Generally, I strive to limit these though because even modest comments can quickly add up to a lot of time.

You said in chapter two that a downside to rubrics is that they can encourage a box-checking mentality on larger papers. How can I guard against that?

If not carefully designed, rubrics can train students to view revision as checking off boxes given by someone else. The way I guard against that is my final rubric category–"The Rest"– which allots a sizeable chunk of points to the other factors that make the paper work or not work. This is an idea I got from famed writing teacher Ken Lindblom (2018), who includes a line in his rubric that simply says, "Is interesting to read." Lindblom adds this because while he likes the way that rubrics demystify grades, he, too, was worried about the things not included in the rubric. According to him this simple category changed everything and got the students thinking about the wider paper in a way that they didn't when they could simply follow the steps outlined in the rubric to a strong grade.

My "The Rest" takes this idea and expands it to anything that may or may not make a paper work. Its language is purposefully more vague and subjective than the phrasing in the rest of the rubric, which lets students know that they need to step back and think about the rest of the factors that could go into how I read it. It reminds them that their language, voice, topic, ideas, tone, and dozens of other things also contribute to whether the piece as a whole works. At the same time, the points given for this category are modest, lowering the stakes for the students who might find the ambiguity alarming.

In the end, I, like Lindblom, have found that having this category and its purposeful ambiguity in conjunction with the clear messages in the rest of the rubric to be the just-right blend to enable me to give lots of clear messages and also have a solid deterrent to box-check-thinking that can turn rubrics from a wonderful communication tool into a liability that inspires uninspired, formulaic writing.

The Rest	– It is well organized and has no sudden transitions.	__/30
	– It has interesting language and a clear and consistent voice.	
	– The topic is compelling and interesting.	
	– The writing in the paper works because . . .	

The Last Word on Effective Feedback

The suggestions made in this chapter enjoy great support from researchers and educators, yet I have personally found adopting many of them to be really difficult. Not fixing or pointing out comma splices for *all* students on *all* papers? Not leaving *any* comments on a final draft? Keeping micro-conferences to *a minute* or less? These all still feel at times more like I am cutting corners than engaging in thoughtful practice.

I, like most teachers I've met, became a teacher of writing because I love helping kids find their voices, I love language, and I loved a few writing teachers I had while in school. And when confronted with something like a comma splice, leaving it alone can feel like we are letting down our students, who will be judged on such things in the world; letting down our beloved language, which we have devoted our lives to celebrating and passing on; and letting down our mentors, many of whom would have unabashedly sliced and diced it with a red pen.

I have found that it is at these times though that we need to be the most diligent. If we give in to such feelings in those micro-moments, and fix everything or let our conferences run over, it can add up to a macro-impact on our ability to engage in effective practices like approaching student work as an interested partner, giving serious formative feedback, translating reactions into actions, and separating feedback and assessment. It can also easily add dozens or even hundreds of hours of extra work over the course of the year—work that is often more likely to lead to serious burnout than serious student growth.

Photo by Isabel Espinosa.

CHAPTER THREE

Making Feedback Memorable
The Feedback Cycle

Before you dig into this chapter, let's start with a quick memory test:

1. What is something you read in the last 24 hours? Anything at all. A book, an article, a poem. Try to remember as much detail as possible.

2. Next, think about something you read last week. What do you remember of that? Try to remember as much of that as you can, too.

3. Last, think about something you read last month. What do you remember of that? Can you even remember specific things you read last month?

If you are like most people, you scored like this: You can likely remember the thing from the last day pretty well, a few scattered bits of the piece from last week, and almost nothing or nothing at all from the piece from last month.

I can predict these results with relative certainty because of a model called the Forgetting Curve, created in 1885 by a psychologist named Hermann Ebbinghaus (see Figure 3.1).

In the Forgetting Curve, we see just how ruthless our brains are when it comes to clearing the memory storehouses of information that doesn't seem relevant anymore. The exact specifics of the curve are hard to define because each person's

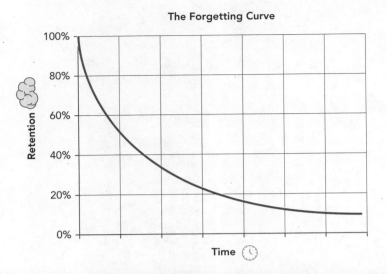

FIGURE 3.1 • The Ebbinghaus Forgetting Curve

memory is different and changes based on the context, but some attributes of memory are agreed on as nearly universal:

- We start forgetting something as soon as we learn it.
- The slope of forgetting is the most intense in the first 24 hours after we've learned something (Beck, 2018).
- Most people remember only a single digit percentage of what they learned a week earlier; within a month it is not uncommon to remember no specifics at all (Campus Wellness, n.d.).

The Forgetting Curve explains why the details of that book you devoured at the beach last summer have vanished from your memory and why entire classes seem to suffer from mass amnesia after a break.

At the same time, it worth noting that our memory and the memories of our students at times work exceptionally well. While that book from over the summer is gone, you may still remember dozens of quotes verbatim from *The Outsiders* a decade or more after teaching it. And while our students may have forgotten what we told them a couple days ago, some of those same students may remember the hundreds of molecules, formulas, and reactions needed to do well on their upcoming AP Chemistry test.

So why is it that sometimes humans forget nearly everything and other times they can engage in extraordinary feats of mental recall? According to the Forgetting Curve, there is a pretty simple explanation: thoughtful repetition.

In the hundreds of studies that have confirmed the Forgetting Curve since it was identified in 1885, all have found that we forget the vast majority of anything encountered once, but if we revisit and retrieve that information in thoughtful ways, our memories suddenly go from Hyde to Jekyll, transforming from sieves to lockboxes. The physiological reason is that our memories don't exist in one spot in our brains; they exist in the connections between neurons, and each time we revisit a memory the connection is strengthened. Further, while any revisiting of a thought, memory, or concept improves the connection and therefore our memory, we can speed our memory generation by

- Spacing out our repetition. Repetition spaced over distinctly different days and learning sessions is more effective than cramming a lot of repetition into a short period of time (Kang, 2016).

- Interleaving the memory, which is where it is connected to other related ideas or concepts. This tends to be more effective than continuously looking at the memory in isolation.

When we engage in repetition and these techniques, the Forgetting Curve turns into something closer to a remembering curve, with our memory improving dramatically with each subsequent revisiting of the information (see Figure 3.2).

Most modern pedagogical practices take this Forgetting Curve into account. Gone are the days where standard practice is to dump information on students once in a lecture or reading and leave the internalization entirely up to them. Instead, most students revisit key ideas, skills, and content in spaced and interleaved ways through projects, discussions, and carefully crafted activities. There is one common glaring exception to this trend of more recursive practice in our classes though: feedback to student writing.

Feedback still largely tends to be delivered in brief, isolated moments to likely be looked at once—if at all—by the students. Rarely is it spoken of again or connected to feedback from previous weeks. This is a major issue because, as Ebbinghaus reminds us, anything not revisited in meaningful ways is almost sure to be forgotten within a week or two. At that point, it doesn't matter how many of the tools and techniques you employ from the first two chapters, your

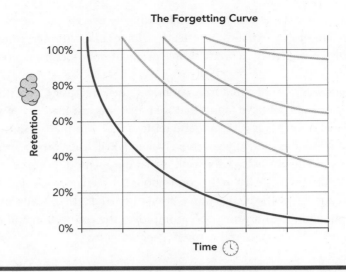

The Forgetting Curve

FIGURE 3.2 • The Ebbinghaus Forgetting Curve, Multiple Revisits

feedback will be largely ineffective and inefficient, with most of the hours you poured into it not translating into student learning.

I know this in part because during my first years in the classroom, I lived it. I only had my students look at my feedback to their writing once, and each successive round of student papers felt almost as if my feedback had never been given. Like some endless and highly frustrating *Groundhog Day* movie plot, my students made most of the same mistakes and I gave them most of the same responses over and over and over.

I've learned from the teachers I've talked with that this experience is hardly unique to me. In fact, frustration over student lack of attention and retention is nearly always one of the first subjects that comes up when I talk to teachers about giving feedback to student writing. At the same time, when I mention the Forgetting Curve—which argues that we need to revisit something more than once to truly learn it—as a potential culprit, the response I get is often a defensive one: The effort and work required to provide feedback to 140, 150, 160, or more students are already too much. Adding more steps to feedback and more things to do in class is just too much to juggle for jugglers who already have so many batons in the air that they are eternally in danger of dropping one.

I completely understand this reaction. I too struggle to keep all the batons in the air and instinctively push back against adding one more thing into my head or into my day. But I also know that I don't want the feedback that I spent many painstaking hours providing to be largely forgotten and that when students don't absorb my feedback, I waste untold hours trying to reteach concepts I'd already covered. Luckily, there is a third way, one that gets students to revisit and dive deeper into feedback in ways that, far from adding to the teacher's load, actually take some work off of their plates: the Feedback Cycle (see Figure 3.3). When we get our students engaging in this cycle, they can't help but revisit our words four, five, six, or more times, maximizing the impact of our lessons and meaning that at times we can give less feedback and still get better results. Here is what each stage of it looks like in my classroom.

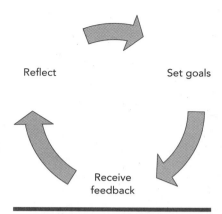

FIGURE 3.3 • The Feedback Cycle

Setting Goals for Improvement

The Feedback Cycle begins with thoughtful goal-setting, which Angela Duckworth (2016) argues in *Grit* is what separates those who accomplish good things from those who accomplish great things in nearly any field. Duckworth asserts that those who start any new step or phase in the pursuit of a much larger goal—such as becoming a champion swimmer or a world-class violinist—by identifying their most significant problem areas and then creating targeted goals aimed at fixing those problem areas vastly outperform those who don't over time because "one by one, these subtle refinements add up to dazzling mastery" (p. 123).

The same principle can and should apply to writing instruction. When students actively engage in assessing their own writing and create thoughtful and deliberate goals, the result is indeed dazzling, largely because the goals students set require them to revisit feedback they have previously received from their teachers, peers, and self—something even the most committed students rarely do in the day-to-day bustle of the school year. When one views this through the lens of the Forgetting Curve, these moments of revisiting previous feedback will lead to more lessons from that feedback learned and learned deeper. Further, we as teachers don't have to do anything to get this increased impact but prompt the students to make goals. Once again, no additional papers need go home with us.

This increased impact of our feedback is likely a large part of why out of the thousands of teaching practices he analyzed, John Hattie lists student goal setting and monitoring of those goals as the practice with highest impact, one that can potentially *triple* the speed of student learning (Fisher, Frey, & Hattie, 2018). Deliberate goal setting is also the only practice directly identified by Hattie and two of the other biggest meta-studies of writing instruction this century: "Writing Next" by the Carnegie Corporation (Graham & Perin, 2007) and "Critical Factors for Success in the 21st Century" by SRI International (2018) in conjunction with the U.S. Department of Education.

> "We have to do this work with the students, and not for the students."
>
> –Patty McGee

The trick with goal setting, however, is that it is not as simple as telling students to set goals. When I first started asking students to set writing goals, many of them struggled to come up with anything, and the goals students did create tended to be vague, broad, superficial, and overall not great. Further, the students tended to forget the goals they set almost as quickly as they set them.

Patty McGee (2017) also identifies these issues in her book *Feedback That Moves Writers Forward*, and consequently she spends a great deal of time looking at what separates high-impact goals from those that have little to no impact. In the end, her examination boils down to what she calls the "Three Cs":

- Clarity
- Challenge
- Commitment

CLARITY: SENTENCE STEMS AND TEACHER MODELING

For many students setting their own goals is a completely new concept. Until now, many have relied solely on teachers to set all the writing goals, so when given the opportunity to do it themselves they are unsure of how to set a goal or what value it has.

For example, a number of goals I got in my early attempts at goal setting looked something like these:

- "I want to be more focused."
- "I want to have more voice."

- "I want better organization."
- "I want to improve my grammar."

Goals like these sound nice on the surface, but they don't actually mean much. These broad statements don't provide a clear path for how the goal will be executed or what it will look like when it is done. Goals like these are sort of like a construction crew opening a blueprint and finding the words: "Please build a nice house."

Consequently, if we want student goals to be better, we need to teach them how to set clear, specific goals. When we first start setting goals in my classroom, I model what the difference is between vague goals and clear goals. Figure 3.4 shows a few of the models I give.

The other way I help them be specific is to give students sentence stems to fill in early in the year in the same way that McGee (2017) does. Stems can be controversial, because they can limit the students' voices. Yet I have found that in the context of early goal setting, sentence stems open more opportunities than they limit because they push students to give those specifics and destinations

VAGUE GOALS	CLEAR GOALS
I want to have more focus.	I've noticed that my writing tends to drift into topics that are only barely related to my central topic. In this paper, I plan to work on improving my focus by creating a clear outline that will keep me focused.
I want to have more voice.	I've noticed that my voice often feels flat in my writing. I want to make my voice feel more alive by substituting clichés for more unique language. I plan to do this by doing a read for clichés once I do the first draft.
I want to have better organization.	I've noticed that I tend to repeat myself or jump from one topic to another in ways that can confuse my reader. I hope to fix this in this paper by having each paragraph begin with a clear topic sentence that I will use to keep myself organized.
I want to have better grammar.	I've noticed that I have a lot of comma errors, especially regarding not adding commas when I should. I plan to better learn the comma rules and then do a read of the final draft where I label on the page what rule each comma I include follows.

FIGURE 3.4 • Vague vs. Clear Goals

needed for goals to have real impact. Below is the stem I give to help students set goals at the start of the unit. I used to have students put it into their writer's notebooks and then I would jot their goals down, but I now have students fill this out digitally using a Google Form, which allows the students and me to have instant access to it whenever we want.

> *I've noticed that [name an issue in my writing]. On this paper, I plan to work on [fill in the skill or attribute of writing that will improve the issue] by [give specific actions or targets].*

I have found modeling in combination with using stems can help even the weakest goal setters craft clear and deliberate goals almost instantly.

CHALLENGE:
MICRO-CONFERENCES TO PUSH LEARNING

In a discussion of goal setting, John Hattie (2012) argues, "Students often set safe targets. . . . Our job is to mess that up. . . . Our job is to help them exceed what they think they can do." In other words, students are like the rest of us: Far too often they discount what they can do, avoid excess effort, and fear uncertain outcomes, so they tend toward setting safe goals, especially if the goals are connected to a grade or even just connected to a teacher who will grade them at some point.

Our job, as Hattie suggests, is indeed to push students out of this comfortable, safe zone and toward goals that challenge them. I do this by holding micro-conferences with students after they submit their goals. I aim for 15 to 60 seconds for each conference, depending on if redirection or nudging is needed. In these conferences, it is important not to steer students' choices too heavily because for goals to be authentic, they need to be self-created. Instead, we can listen to the logic behind each goal and look for places where we can affirm student choices and places where we can nudge them to go further. My goal for micro-conferences is to get to a place where student goals are, to use a term from video game designers, "optimally challenging," which means they are difficult enough not to be boring yet not so difficult that they produce excess anxiety. Also, I do my best to not completely redirect the students unless a goal is completely off-base. Setting goals is all about empowering students, and there are few things less empowering than a teacher using student goal setting to push his own objectives. Students will get teacher goals soon enough, but this first stage is all about inviting the students to have a say, which will yield great learning dividends.

COMMITMENT: REVISITING
GOALS AS THE UNIT PROGRESSES

When students have a say, they tend to be committed to their goals—at the start. But commitment may wane as the unit moves on. This is an issue because to meet a goal in any endeavor or discipline, we generally need our commitment to remain firm.

The key to helping students maintain their commitment to their goals is we need to stay committed to their goals as well. This is why it's important to regularly make time for students to revisit and think about the goals; if we don't, goals may quickly get forgotten and ultimately have little or no impact on student growth. For my part, I have three times where I directly ask students to think through and revisit their goals:

- Peer response

- A self-review checklist they complete in the early revision stages

- Our conference concerning their penultimate draft

(For those looking for more specifics on these, we look more in depth at peer response and self-review in Chapter 5 and conferencing later in this chapter.)

In each one of these moments where students revisit their goals—or at any other time for that matter—students have the option to change, tweak, or amend their goals in a Google Form because, as Patty McGee (2017) reminds us:

> [T]he goals our young writers start with are likely not the goals with which they will end. Along the way, and often as a result of feedback, goals evolve, becoming more tailored, traveling in different directions, being replaced altogether, or giving birth to [other] goals. (p. 144)

If a student asks to change a goal, I ask her to go back and fill out the goal setting Google Form again, which stays up and live on my site. This allows the student to reassess and revisit goals in meaningful ways whenever needed and takes some pressure off the initial goal setting,

The other way I commit to student goals is I add them to the final rubric (see Figure 3.5). Points are assigned based on students' own commitment and effort in the pursuit of the goal.

CATEGORY	CRITERIA	POINTS POSSIBLE
Make Me Care	– It has uncertainty and serious stakes that create tension. – It contains a lot of specific details and imagery. – It uses almost all indirect characterization. – The words are carefully chosen and emotional. – You feel like you know the author; it has minimal cliché usage.	__/20
Story Arc	– The setting grabs the reader and makes a promise that this will be worth his/her/their time; it contains interesting questions. – There is a clear problem that builds to a climax; the climax has tension and is some of your best writing. – The resolution ties up all the loose ends; if no resolution is present, there is a good reason for it.	__/10
Grammar	– All commas are used correctly. – There is interesting use of advanced grammatical techniques to enhance the piece. – There are no nonpurposeful run-ons and fragments. – The grammar is polished according to Standard English conventions (or has good reasons for why it doesn't follow the conventions).	__/10
Mr. Johnson's Growth Areas	You spend time grappling with Mr. Johnson's core growth areas; you move forward in those areas in significant ways. Mr. Johnson's core growth areas for me include (1) (2)	__/15
Your Goals	You put serious effort toward improving in your goal areas. Your personal goals are (1) (2)	__/15
The Rest	– It is well organized and has no sudden transitions. – It has interesting language and a clear and consistent voice. – The topic is compelling and interesting. – The writing in the paper works because . . .	__/30
Total	Comments:	__/100

FIGURE 3.5 • Personal Essay Criteria, With Focus on Students' Goals

Student goals are powerful. Goals help students revisit feedback; serve as a bridge between the work that came before and the upcoming work; empower students by framing their education as a joint venture between the teacher and the student where we both must turn the key to engage the learning; and introduce the three core traits needed for someone to develop intrinsic motivation: autonomy (they get some say), purpose (they can in part pursue what matters to them), and mastery (they can pick goals that while challenging feel within reach) (Pink, 2009). And they do it all without us having to grade a single other paper.

Receiving Feedback Through Conferences

Feedback given but not heard doesn't lead to gains, and feedback heard but not revisited rarely results in serious long-term learning. We do have a tool, though, to ensure that our feedback is heard, remembered, and revisited in a deep way: conferences.

> "Conferences humanize teaching."
>
> –Kelly Gallagher and Penny Kittle, *180 Days*

Conferences are among the most commonly suggested and deeply beloved pedagogical tools that I know. They are the nucleus of the workshop model and the focus of a great many books on writing instruction, yet conferences remain relatively rare in secondary classrooms. The majority of teachers with whom I've had candid conversations have admitted to me, often in whispered tones, that they do little to no conferencing.

Why should I make the time for conferences?

The reasons for the enthusiastic, nearly unanimous chorus in support of conferencing are real–and compelling:

- Conferences are a place to discover and patch inevitable misunderstandings, misconceptions, and miscommunications.

- Each student brings a unique understanding of writing informed by all the writing and writing instruction that came before. Conferences allow us a clear picture of how students view and know writing. And remember, we strive to teach the writer, not the writing.

(Continued)

(Continued)

- Conferences invite students to be active partners in a way that even the most welcoming written comments cannot, which allows them to gain agency over their learning.
- Personal conversations offer the students context and clarification.
- Conferences allow an unparalleled opportunity to build real and meaningful relationships with students. When they feel they have a strong relationship with a teacher, students work harder, listen closer, and feel safer to take the thoughtful risks needed for rapid growth. A well-constructed conference can cultivate such relationships shockingly fast.

The reason for this gap between literature and practice often boils down to one thing: Conferencing takes a ton of time. As I mentioned in Chapter 2, each set of 5-minute conferences I engage in equals nearly a week of class time, and when we have pages and pages of standards and binders of content we are expected to cover, it can feel nearly impossible to find that kind of time. Yet conferences are essential to the Feedback Cycle, because they are the place where teachers can ensure that each student truly understands the feedback. Misconceptions and missed lessons regarding our feedback will happen, slowing and scuttling its effectiveness. So, while not easy, we need to make time for conferences if we want our feedback to stick. And it is possible to have really effective conferences fast—in 5 minutes or less—by following some core principles.

PREPARE FOR THE CONFERENCE

Conference expert Carl Anderson (2018) explains that there are three basic parts to a conference:

1. Discovering what the student is doing as a writer

2. Assessing what the student is doing and using that information to prioritize what to teach

3. Teaching the student

Or put simpler, we need to learn, plan, and execute. From a teaching perspective, doing all three of these things well on the fly in 5 minutes is a pretty heavy lift. So how does one accomplish all this in the same time that it takes to warm a microwave burrito? The answer: preparation.

Teacher and writer Julie Patterson (2018) wrote that "conferring isn't improv," a line that has stuck with me. While conferences may look like improv on the surface, the most effective ones generally involve quite a bit of preparation by both students and teachers. This preparation starts with the teacher. I always read and assess the papers I will be discussing ahead of time, because assessing a piece of writing well just isn't possible in the 5-minute average that I strive for. That is why my conferences always come on the heels of comprehensive feedback. The comments I make on student papers become the notes for my conferences with them, saving me another read through their papers. For those who worry as I once did that this might be redundant, remember we learn from attention and repetition. Conferences are a great way to make sure that students are paying close attention, understanding clearly, and revisiting our deepest and most personal feedback—the feedback we've committed dozens of hours to. Further, I don't simply repeat in the conference what I wrote on the paper; the feedback on the paper is a start, and the conference is the opportunity to extend and explain that feedback as the student needs it.

The student preparation comes next. Students bring to the conference answers to a series of reflective questions. The questions I use are roughly based off the questions of Carl Anderson (2018) and veteran writing teacher Dr. Deanna Mascle of Morehead State (2016), with the following being a few of my favorites:

- How would you say the piece is going so far? What have been the biggest struggles with it? What are you really proud of?

- What in my feedback do you understand? What are you struggling with or don't understand? What do you disagree with?

- How are you doing in meeting the goals you have set for yourself? Do you want to shift them?

- What are your needs going forward? What can I do to help you move your paper forward?

It is only after this preparation on both sides that the conferences begin. Between my preparation and the students' preparation, we will have completed Anderson's first two steps of conferencing—reading and assessment/prioritizing. This leaves the teacher just one task—teaching—to do during the conference. Also, it is worth noting that when taking this approach to conferencing, my students revisit my feedback two more times at a minimum, once in their reflection and again at the conference, putting them well down the road toward internalizing the feedback into their long-term memories.

Before moving on, I want to acknowledge that the teaching part of the conference, which comes through one-on-one discussion with the students, does have an element of improv, but like professional improv actors, the moments of great success tend to arise largely from the thoughtful preparation ahead of time.

LEVEL THE INTERACTION

A well-run conference can shift the dynamic of writing in the classroom from one in which the student writes because of and for an audience of one (the teacher) to one where the students and teachers are collaborators in the pursuit of improving the student's skills. I've seen this happen countless times, but it still amazes me to watch students make this transition from writing for their teachers to writing for themselves.

This critical shift doesn't happen simply because we conference though. The approach we take to conferring is critical to whether the ownership of the writing passes to the students or resides with the teacher. There are a few key techniques we can use to encourage this transfer of ownership:

- *Invite students to speak first.* Legendary writing teacher Donald Graves always began a conference by doing what he called "receiving" a piece (Newkirk, 2017). He made sure the students' voices were recognized by having them start the conference. In general, students defer to the teacher's voice, so when we start talking, students respond by trying to say the things they think the teacher wants them to say. In contrast, when the students start the conference and we attentively *receive* their writing and insights, there is a much better chance that students will say what they really think and need. There are many ways that one can do this, but my favorite is the simplest: I begin conferences with some basic variant of the statement, "Tell me about this piece" or "What did your reflection focus on," and I make sure to truly hear and receive the student's words before asking questions and offering suggestions.

- *Use nonverbal cues to encourage a feeling of partnership.* Something as seemingly harmless as having the students take the long walk to the teacher's desk can establish a tone similar to visiting the great and powerful Oz. With that in mind, I always have my conferences at student desks, and I sit next to them to be at the level of the student. I also refer to the paper on the student's computer or paper, even if I have a copy myself. These nonverbal details are subtle and subtextual, but humans are subtle, subtextual creatures. When we meet kids where they are, both literally and figuratively, we signal that this conference is a partnership. I've found these little cues can make a large difference in the tenor of the conversation.

- *Ask more questions.* We teachers have so much that we want to *tell* each student that when given the rare opportunity to talk to them, it's easy to slip into lecture or story-telling mode. Yet we don't want our narrative to take over the conference or else a conference becomes little more than live-action readings of written feedback. While our perspective is key to the conference, the student's is as well. I approach each conference with the unwritten goal to tally more questions asked than answers offered.

DOCUMENT THE CONFERENCE

Conferencing experts make the case that we should take notes during our conferences (Anderson, 2018). There is no other way that we will remember what we talked about in each individual conference weeks and months later, and having those notes can be valuable for

- Helping us see how the students are (or aren't) evolving and shifting
- Making trends in student writing clearer
- Ensuring we aren't redundant
- Data collection purposes for administrators, parents or guardians, and special education teachers
- Lesson planning

It isn't easy to take notes during a conference though. Too much time writing during the conference detracts from the interaction, making it feel more like an interview or an interrogation than a collaborative conversation. At the same time, we need notes that are complete and accurate enough that they will make sense to us weeks and months later. Figure 3.6 shows an example of my conference notes.

Here are the key details about how these notes are constructed and used.

- Conference notes are organized by student, not date. Organizing by date would mean the information about each student would be scattered throughout my conference binder. Instead, I have a sheet for each student in a conference binder that I put together at the start

Student Name: Sophie

DATE	STUDENT QUESTIONS/ CONCERNS	TOPICS DISCUSSED	ACTION STEPS
9/19	• Unclear on linking verbs • Not sure how to make it longer	• Conjugations of "to be" • Imagery • Details/indirect characterization	• Have fewer than five "to bes" per page on average • More indirect characterization than direct characterization
10/30	• Having trouble adding more depth • Wants to improve sentence structure/ flow	• Sentence length variation and types of sentences • Levels of generality	• Add at least two more sentences to each body paragraph • Have more longer sentences by adding more detail/sentence combining
12/12	• Wants to improve punctuation, especially colons and semicolons • Word choice	• Being personal with word choice • Colons/ semicolon rules • Comma splices	• No punctuation errors and at least one thoughtful colon/ semicolon • More engaging intro and conclusion

FIGURE 3.6 • Conference Notes

of the year. While it can be a pain to print and collate pages for each student at the start of the year, the half hour invested allows me to see within seconds the progression of that student for the rest of the year, and for me that is an investment that makes sense.

- The notes are already divided into three categories:

    o Student questions and concerns

    o Major topics

    o Action steps

    I've found breaking the information into these categories helps me quickly access the information that is the most likely to be needed while I am conferencing.

- My notes are handwritten. Nearly everything else I do is digital, because it is faster and generally easier to organize. But when it comes to conferencing I find that the glowing wall of the computer screen makes a conference feel more formal and intimidating, while a regular old notebook tends to blend into the desk and be forgotten by the student.

- My goal with the notes isn't to be a stenographer; it is simply to have a rough sketch of the key moments that can jog my memory about previous sections. That is why I don't write down everything; I just write the key things.

Reflecting on What's Been Accomplished . . . and What's Yet to Master

Arthur L. Costa and Bena Kallick (2008) argue in *Learning Through Reflection* that

> [m]ost classrooms are oriented more to the present and the future than to the past. Such an orientation means that students (and teachers) find it easier to discard what has happened and to move on without taking stock of the seemingly isolated experiences of the past. (para. 11)

This description matches my experience as both a student and teacher over the last 30 years. While schools talk a lot about the importance of reflection, actual moments of reflection are rare throughout the school day. Instead, the horizon, containing the next lesson or the next paper, tends to be the priority. Reflection, if there is time, is sometimes given a tertiary role, but those reflective moments tend to be largely momentary and fleeting, little more than a quick glance backward before pushing ever onward.

This diminished role of reflection is a serious problem because, according to our Forgetting Curve, revisiting and thinking about something we've already learned—or, in other words, reflecting on it—is largely what separates what we remember from what we forget. This is why reflection is a crucial part of the Feedback Cycle. If goal setting gets students assessing their writing skills and gaps and conferencing ensures they receive and think closely about our feedback, reflection is where a great deal of those lessons turn into lasting learning. It is also where they determine what they might still need to learn, priming them for the next round of goal setting and trip through the Feedback Cycle.

This is why we need to elevate reflection by building in regular, serious moments of it into our classes. Here are some ways to do that.

STUDENT SELF-ASSESSMENT AS REFLECTION

As discussed in Chapter 2, final drafts in my classes get no or few comments from me because I pour the majority of my commenting resources into earlier formative drafts. But this doesn't mean that they are lacking in written feedback. The written feedback instead comes from the students, who reflect for 5 to 10 minutes on what grade they deserve right before they turn in their papers. This activity is hugely important for the approach I take to feedback because:

1. Self-assessment offers students a meaningful opportunity to reflect and thereby deepen the internalization of the key lessons of the unit. Further, students tend to take it seriously because this isn't some abstract exercise. A real audience will be reading it for a real purpose.

2. Most students are remarkably thoughtful and clear-headed about their strengths and weaknesses, with their core insights mirroring mine more than one might expect. Thus, when students respond to their own papers, they can accurately replace the feedback we teachers cannot give on final drafts because of time concerns. This also allows us, if we want to give comments on final drafts, to affirm students' observations, which takes a fraction of the time of trying to write full

comments and reinforces their discovery. Remember, when learners are solving their own problems, the learning will be more memorable.

3. Students and teachers won't always agree, and self-assessment reflections will flush out areas where students might be confused and/or disagree with the teacher's final assessment. Knowing the areas of confusion or disagreement in advance gives us a better understanding of when we need to jump in with written feedback or a short conference about a final draft instead of simply filling out a rubric.

The way we go about the self-assessment reflection is simple. The students fill out the co-constructed rubric and then write a 5-minute reflection on the paper. Here is the prompt I give them.

Please fill out the rubric with the scores you believe the final draft should receive. Once you finish doing that, please write a short reflection at the bottom about how you think the paper turned out and why you gave it the scores you gave. In this reflection please answer the following:

- *How did the paper turn out? What are the major highlights and what were the major struggles?*

- *What areas did you give high scores? Why? Give specific reasons to support those high marks.*

- *What areas got some of the lowest scores? Why did those get lower scores and what can you do next time to improve in these areas?*

- *What else should I know about when scoring the paper?*

END OF UNIT REFLECTION

Each unit in my class ends with a reflection in which the students think back on their goals, the focus areas identified in my feedback, and their final paper. I use a Google Form to collect these (see Figure 3.7), because I find it harder for the students and me to lose, but the same questions could be done on a printed-out sheet or in a writer's notebook.

There are two important things to note about this reflection. First, it puts students in the role of collecting and recording feedback. The teacher does not have to record or keep track of anything. The students will compile and give the

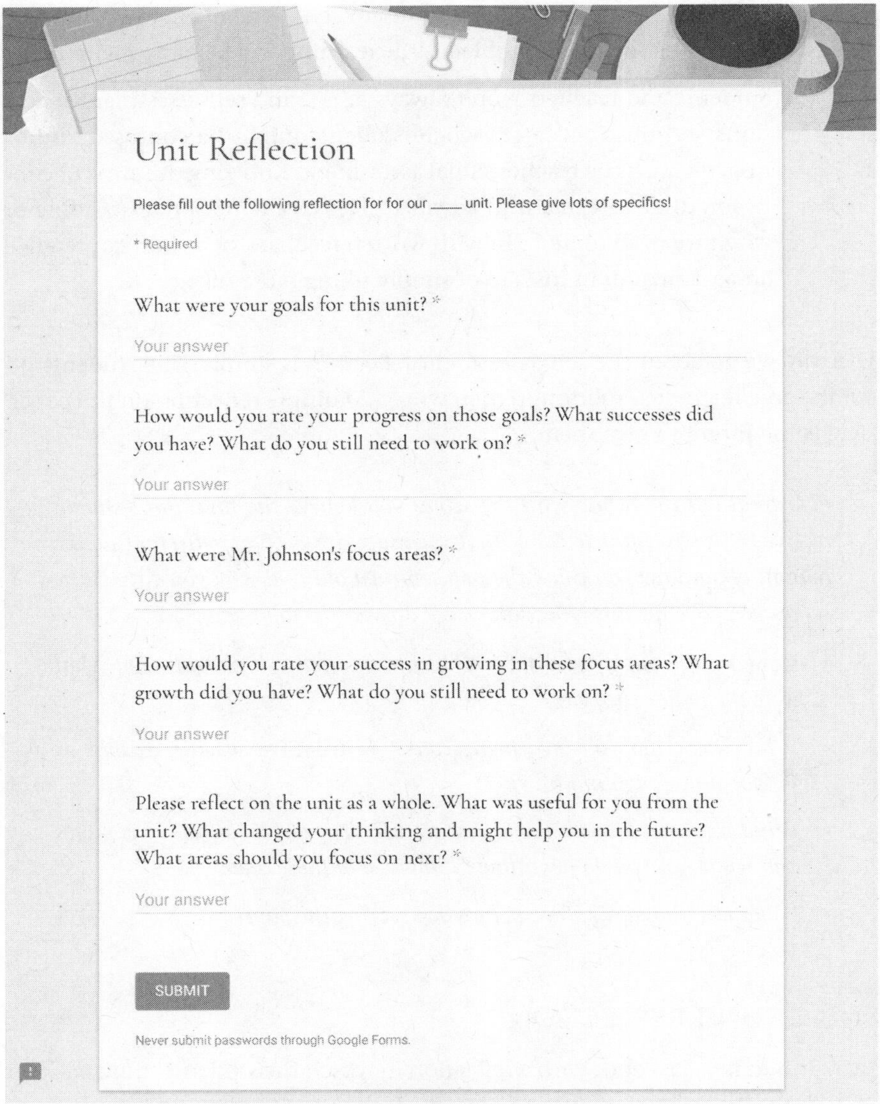

Unit Reflection

Please fill out the following reflection for for our ____ unit. Please give lots of specifics!

* Required

What were your goals for this unit? *

Your answer

How would you rate your progress on those goals? What successes did you have? What do you still need to work on? *

Your answer

What were Mr. Johnson's focus areas? *

Your answer

How would you rate your success in growing in these focus areas? What growth did you have? What do you still need to work on? *

Your answer

Please reflect on the unit as a whole. What was useful for you from the unit? What changed your thinking and might help you in the future? What areas should you focus on next? *

Your answer

SUBMIT

Never submit passwords through Google Forms.

FIGURE 3.7 • End (and Beginning) of Unit Reflection

teacher a digital list of the key pieces of feedback from the unit that the teacher and student can access anytime. Second, while I give this to students at the end of each unit, this moment actually marks the beginning of the next unit, because the students' endpoints tend to be wonderful places to start the goals for the next unit—the Feedback Cycle continues.

LETTER WRITING

This is an idea that I got from Tracy Anderson (2006), author of *Purposeful Writing* and a dear colleague who teaches down the hall at my school. Every quarter, Tracy has her students write a letter to her about how they are doing as people and students. Figure 3.8 shows an example of the format.

I have also included a series of downloadable letter prompts on the companion website at **resources.corwin.com/flashfeedback**.

The idea behind this is simple, but the results are remarkable. While it never uses the word *reflection,* what this assignment does (beyond provide a treasure-trove of information about each student's evolving interests, mindset, and reaction to the class) is it gets them reflecting on the lessons and assignments from the class. To further encourage them to revisit specific lessons and assignments, I give students class time and suggest that they take out their writer's notebook,

---

QUARTER TWO LETTER

Our first quarter is already in the books, and I want to hear how it went. For the first assignment of the second quarter, please write me a roughly one-page letter covering the following topics:

- **How are you doing?** What have been the most interesting and exciting parts of your life this quarter? What accomplishments or goals have you reached since September? What aspirations and dreams do you have for the next quarter?

- **How are you doing with your writing?** How have you grown as a writer since the beginning of the course? What specific triumphs have you had? Where are you still struggling as a writer? What do you hope to learn about writing in the next quarter?

- **How are you doing with your reading?** What books have you read this fall? What books are next? How have you felt about the books covered in class? What were your favorites? Which ones did you not connect to as much?

In the letter, you do not need to answer every question and can feel free to organize the letter any way that you want. Also, I am definitely more interested in specifics than vague answers (for example, don't just say, "I'm a better writer." Instead say something like, "I realized that I used mostly short sentences, which made my writing choppy. In my narrative, I did a much better job of varying my sentences, which I think gave it a smoother feel!").

FIGURE 3.8 • A Letter Example

previous papers, or conference notes to help with constructing the letter. I also place letters right after major assignments so that they act as an additional layer of reflection that solidifies the learning from that assignment. Figure 3.9 shows two excerpts of recent student letters. Notice how the letters revisit my feedback and instruction and weave them together with their own experiences

---

STUDENT LETTER EXCERPT #1:

A lot of what the class has taught me is confidence in my writing. By knowing the things I should focus on—to be, clichés, sentence length—I don't stare blankly at a paper wondering what to fix. I have a purpose in my editing process, asking myself questions like, "do I have parallel structure?" as opposed to open ended broad ones like, "Is it good?" Understanding why writing appeals to an audience changes what I strive to write and how I get there.

Similar to many of my other pursuits, I need to dedicate more of my time to the writing process if I'm going to get better. Again I feel like I've made some great strides, and it's shown in papers here and in other classes, but I'm still missing that 3rd or 4th reread and edit cycle to really iron out final kinks. I really hate reading things I've already written, because hey, I wrote it so obviously I know what's going on. That's a vice I'm going to have to get over for the second half of this class if I want to take a next step.

STUDENT LETTER EXCERPT #2:

Quite honestly, my writing has improved a lot; my best piece of writing so far is my personal essay. I would say my biggest issue coming into this class was grammar and choppy writing because that was what has been said by other teachers. After this first quarter, I started making conscious decisions on sentence length; I began looking where I can split very long sentences and combine sentences where it started getting too choppy. I've realized how sentence structure creates rhythm and flow to writing because whenever I write I listen to music. If music had the same beat and flow without variation then it would become pretty boring to listen to, so with that in mind let the music that I'm listening to while writing carry me. All in all, I would say my biggest upgrade in writing so far is my varying sentence length.

The thing I need to improve the most is depth. I tend to mention things but not go in-depth. When I do write with a lot of depth and detail it comes out good, but for the majority of my writing, I don't go in-depth. On my personal essay feedback, it mentioned this and the second thing I need to improve the most is clarity. Sometimes I write in a way that I will get but no one else will understand. In a piece of writing that is being read by someone else, it needs to be understood by them if it is not then you need to improve in your clarity. I will always understand my writing but I need to work on how to make understandable to others.

FIGURE 3.9 • Student Mid-Semester Letters

and observations—exactly in the way that the Ebbinghaus Forgetting Curve says we should to maximize our learning.

THE REFLECTION PAPER

Part of my final semester grade for each student is a paper called the Reflection Paper. It is exactly what it sounds like—a reflection on the entire semester—and I find it to be the single most effective assessment of what a student has learned. This paper is more than just an assessment though; it also serves as an instructional tool that spans the entire semester.

The key to getting high-quality reflection papers that act as both meaningful assessments and learning tools is to hand out a sheet prefacing the assignment early. I do this on the second day of class because I want to establish the central role of reflection in the classroom and separate my class from other classes where reflection is talked up but rarely done. Giving the assignment early also sets up an incentive for students to diligently do the regular reflections listed above. Figure 3.10 shows the sheet I hand out on the second day of school; it is available for download from the companion website at **resources.corwin .com/flashfeedback**.

THE REFLECTION PAPER

Reflection is the fire in which real learning is forged. If we don't think closely and critically about our practice in anything we do—ranging from basketball to playing piano—our growth tends to happen at a snail's pace. On the other hand, when we reflect on how we are changing, our growth tends to be turbo-charged.

With that in mind, throughout the semester you will be given many moments to track and reflect on your growth. These observations and reflections will turn into the final assignment of the year, which is a thoughtful two-to-three-page paper where you examine where your writing started this semester, how you grew as a writer over the semester, and where you need to go next now that your semester is over.

This paper will be graded largely on the following:

How Specific It Is

I will be looking for specific details, stories, and examples. This means instead of saying something like, "I learned to have smoother writing," I will expect you to say something like, "I realized in my first paper that I used the same kind of sentence

(Continued)

(Continued)

over and over, which made my writing feel repetitive. Having more varied sentence types was my key goal for much of the first two papers, and by the third paper, my sentence variety had gone from a problem to a strength!"

How Deep It Is

I will also be looking for you to fully explain each point you made. This means that instead of just saying your word choice is better, you will explain how you accomplished that. Did you pay closer attention to the sounds of your words or give it an extra read during revision for places to add playful or unusual wording?

How Accurate It Is

The last big thing I will be assessing this paper on is its accuracy. Do you have a good sense of the actual successes you had, struggles you went through, focus areas you grew in, and spots where you still need to improve?

FIGURE 3.10 • The Reflection Paper

The Last Word on Memorable Feedback

Feedback is commonly viewed as something that comes from us, the teacher, after something is done or nearly done, likely because feedback by definition is a response that someone gives to something, and it is difficult to respond to something that doesn't exist yet. To approach feedback this way though—as simply *our* response—will inevitably lead to chopping it up into stand-alone lessons, likely dooming most of the feedback we poured hundreds of hours into over the semester to be forgotten. This is because it cuts out the student, whose continued revisiting and attention is what will ultimately divide lessons learned from lessons forgotten.

Instead, we need to treat each piece of feedback as what it really is: a moment of connection with the students that continues a process that began the first time a student touched a pen to a paper and continues with each successive line written. When we do this and make spaces in our class for our students to do it with us, our feedback, its efficacy, and our students' voices and memory are all elevated, opening the door to do higher levels of learning in less time than we ever thought possible.

CHAPTER FOUR

Beyond the Text
Using Feedback to Cultivate Positive Mindsets and Beliefs

It was not long ago that traits like determination, motivation, emotional intelligence, and someone's mindset were viewed as largely fixed in the same way that eye or hair color is. Both teachers and the wider society often just assumed that some students were driven, gritty, or cared and some didn't and there was only so much that could be done about it.

In recent years though, it has become clear that nearly any trait or mindset that we'd want to cultivate in our students—ranging from tenacity to motivation—can be taught or bolstered by circumstances (Farrington et al., 2012). Further, study after study has found that improving certain social and emotional traits, skills, and mindsets in students can have a massive impact on the speed and quality of student learning. A few of the most eye-popping include

- A recent McKinsey report found a student's mindset to be *twice* as predictive of test scores as their home background (Mourshed, Krawitz, & Dorn, 2017).

- A 2009 study of ninth graders with low expectations for themselves in their science classes found that when these students wrote one to two paragraphs each month about how the topics from class tied to their lives (versus a control where the students simply wrote monthly summaries), the grade point averages of the class rose by nearly a point and the grade gap between black and white students shrank by 65% (Hulleman, Kosovich, Barron, & Daniel, 2017).

- One very regularly cited study of students in Massachusetts middle schools found that students did *double* the revisions on an essay when they each received a sticky note on the top of their essays that read "I'm giving you these comments because I have very high expectations and I know that you can reach them," versus those who got a sticky note that read "I'm giving you these comments so that you'll have feedback on your paper" (Tough, 2016).

Results like these have a great many social science researchers now stating that social and emotional traits like self-control, resilience, persistence, and drive might be as important as traditional measures like aptitude when it comes to learning (Farrington et al., 2012). Practitioners are also starting to take notice, led in part by Dave Stuart Jr., a teacher from Cedar Springs, Michigan, who makes this research practical in his book *These Six Things* (2018). Stuart synthesizes it into five key beliefs that we as teachers should strive to cultivate in our students—credibility, belonging, efficacy, effort, and value—and he introduces this idea with the following appeal:

> I'd like to argue that all of our work in and out of the classroom ought to be informed by a fundamental layer: the layer of key beliefs. The best kinds of classrooms rely on inside-out learning; they cultivate the right kinds of beliefs in students . . . setting the table, as it were, for the feasts of learning we hope to provide our students. (p. 21)

While Stuart's assertion that learning the "outside" material of the classroom happens best when the student's inside condition is carefully cultivated may not be new, his placement of it as the fundamental layer is an important development. Even many champions of grit and growth mindsets haven't gone so far as to say that learning starts with beliefs and mindsets, but I've found in my experience as an educator that this is exactly where it belongs. I've also found no location to be as fertile for cultivating desired mindsets and beliefs as the feedback we give to students. Here's why:

- Mindsets and beliefs are personal and often need one-on-one personal cultivation to truly flourish. From September to June, we spend more time conversing individually with students in their work than anywhere else.

- New mindsets and beliefs aren't generally formed in 1 day; they need regular reinforcement and practice to stick. Our response to student work is one of the most regular features of the class, meaning we can cultivate a mindset or belief we desire with relative regularity if we embed it into our feedback.

- Teacher responses to their previous work are likely responsible for the formation of much of our students' current positive and negative mindsets and beliefs, making it a powerful place to refashion any negative ones.

Additionally, there is no area of our teaching practice likely to benefit more from students having the right mindsets and beliefs than our feedback. Positive beliefs and mindsets aid in the receiving, remembering, and acting upon feedback because

- Criticism naturally invites defensiveness. While having the right beliefs and mindsets won't completely eliminate defensiveness, they can act as a firewall to keep that defensiveness from affecting students' ability to receive and act on the feedback.

- As was established in earlier chapters, feedback not read, thought about, and acted on—no matter how well framed—generally has little to no impact. The right beliefs and mindset can make it exponentially more likely that students will pay the attention needed to internalize our feedback.

- Writing is one of the hardest and scariest things we ask students to do in school. The moments that challenge and push us out of our comfort zones are the exact moments where we tend to lean on our core beliefs and mindsets the hardest.

Interestingly, despite all we know about the impact of positive mindsets and beliefs, it is rare for teachers to address these things in their responses to student writing. The likely reason is pretty simple: We already have a lot to do in our feedback. There are so many lessons to be taught and, as we have already established, it is essential that we don't overload students with too many comments. Further, each additional minute we add to our average response to a round of student papers adds 2 to 3 additional hours of response time for every paper assigned, meaning we often don't have the time to add *more*, even if it's really good stuff.

Yet we know that shifting a student's mindsets and beliefs about learning can transform that student's work and overall trajectory as a learner, putting us in a dilemma: Do we add more work to our plates by taking on one more element in our feedback, or do we protect ourselves at the expense of a golden teaching opportunity?

Luckily, we don't need to actually answer this question because there exists a middle path where teachers can work on students' beliefs and mindsets in meaningful ways within feedback without adding serious time to their own workload. There is even a name for practices that do exactly that: wise interventions.

Wise Interventions to
Turn Around Problematic Mindsets

Wise interventions are defined as practices that have the ability to shift how people think or behave in mere moments by being highly precise with their targeting and timing. To see one in action, you have to look no further than the sticky note study mentioned at the start of the chapter. Writing a sticky note takes no more than a few extra seconds, yet it yielded double the effort on the students' revisions.

This chapter revolves around such wise interventions and other equally wise and efficient best practices that we can use to make positive and significant changes to our students' mindsets and beliefs—while also being mindful of how we're spending our own time. Like the Feedback Cycle in Chapter 3, positive mindsets and beliefs act as multipliers that will give each piece of our feedback more impact because the students are far better positioned to receive them. This ultimately allows us to give less feedback at times while still getting stronger results, and it means far fewer moments of time-intensive reteaching of concepts.

Wise interventions work so well and quickly because they target the areas in which problematic mindsets and beliefs are created or perpetuated and then disrupt their creation or continuation at just the right moment. Because wise interventions start by identifying the problem areas, we start there, too, by examining the most common problematic student mindsets when it comes to receiving feedback about writing. Then we look at the precise interventions and practices that can declaw negative mindsets and beliefs and replace them with new ones that will turbocharge our students' growth.

"Writing Is Scary": Feedback to Decrease Students' Fear of Writing

Writing is scary for nearly anyone. For example, I have been writing publicly for over a decade, yet even as I write this sentence I am nervous because

- My words are orphans; I am not there to clarify their meaning or defend their honor. They must speak without me.

- The words and ideas here are public and permanent. They are me set in amber for others to judge, a monument to my imperfection in this moment.

- I can never be sure how my writing will be received. As far as I know, no writer has figured out the magic formula for how to always predict with accuracy how an audience will respond to the words on the page or how to make every single sentence a winner.

- Writing can be easily compared. Once set down, my words can be instantly compared to everything else ever written.

Our students face these same fears, and for many these worries weigh far more heavily because the students don't have a history of writing success to lean on when these worries come knocking. Instead, as I mentioned in Chapter 2, a great many students come into my classes with rocky, complicated, or downright painful writing histories. Many of them come nursing festering wounds borne from acute moments of literary trauma, and others who have no specific moments of trauma may still bring long histories of low grades and even lower self-esteem. Or the opposite: They carry fear over what a mistake will do to their grade, which will in turn affect their GPAs and future options.

The combination of how universally scary writing is and the baggage a great many of our students bring can manifest itself in a number of negative behaviors in our students:

- *Diminished effort*: As teachers, we see students every day whose fear acts as a restraint, holding them back from truly trying. This is often because we all, including those students who will readily call themselves dumb or bad at school, generally view ourselves as special or above average at some level. Failure challenges this belief, and so as a preemptive protection we steer a wide berth around locations where the narrative of us being above average could be challenged.

- *Decreased clarity of thought*: The book *The Teaching Brain* (2014) by Vanessa Rodriguez argues that "when a student's working memory is constrained by negative emotion (such as stress, anger, fear, depression, etc.) he will not be able to think as clearly or remember as well" (p. 60). The reason for this is that fear (or stress or anger) causes our amygdala, the brain's fear sensor, to hijack the brain, shutting down the pathways to the prefrontal cortex and pouring all our neurological resources into our fight or flight response (Hamilton, 2015). This may be a good thing from a survival standpoint, but from an academic standpoint, it is a disaster. When the amygdala shuts down those pathways to the prefrontal cortex, our ability to make complex decisions, reason, understand other perspectives, and form and recall memories are all severely limited, making students who truly fear writing physically incapable of writing well or learning until those feelings subside.

- *Outright avoidance.* For students who fear writing the most, perceived writing failures can lead to withdrawing from writing in the classroom altogether. These students often produce nothing or next to nothing and miss deadline after deadline, even after we push, prod, nudge, cut deals, and dangle carrots in front of them. For these students, a zero, a frank discussion with the teacher, or a call home would all likely be unpleasant, but still preferable to the embarrassment and shame that they feel about their writing.

> "We're often told that the key to learning is to get out of our comfort zones, but these findings contradict that particular chestnut: Take us very far out of our comfort zones, and our brains stop paying attention to anything other than surviving the experience. It's clear that we learn most in our comfort zones."
>
> –Marcus Buckingham & Ashley Goodall, *Harvard Business Review*

Decreasing the amount of fear in writing is a tricky thing because whether you are a sixth grader working on your first full essay or Stephen King working on his 50th book, writing is never going to feel 100% safe because it isn't 100% safe. People do judge others on their writing, misunderstand what we believe to be our clearest prose, and our words are left to fend for themselves in the big, wide world. But when teachers use the following wise interventions and practices—none of which take more than a few seconds—the danger of writing can be mitigated enough for nearly all students to steer around the issues of avoidance and amygdalas, leading to massive gains in performance and time saved for both the students and us.

REBRAND FAILURE WITH DIRECT LABELING

The Art of Possibility (2000) by Rosamund Stone Zander and Benjamin Zander begins with a classic joke:

A shoe factory sends two marketing scouts to a region of Africa to study the prospects for expanding business. One sends back a telegram saying, "SITUATION HOPELESS STOP NO ONE WEARS SHOES." The other writes back triumphantly, "GLORIOUS BUSINESS OPPORTUNITY STOP THEY HAVE NO SHOES." (p. 9)

The punchline and the lesson are the same: We often see what we expect to see in the world. Those with entrepreneurial mindsets see opportunities around every corner, and those who are more pessimistic see an endless series of hurdles that will add up to inevitable failure.

Unfortunately, what a great many students see when a new writing assignment flutters down on their desks is the latter, and in this they are partially correct. They will fail, in that vast majority of the writing process is failing and then cleaning up mistakes. Even the best writers spend vastly more time spilling unseemly messes on the page than moments where fluid and eloquent prose effortlessly pour out.

If one approaches writing with a mindset of expected failure, all those moments where words don't come out quite right could serve as solid evidence to support one's inability. This is why before students put a pen to paper or keys to a keyboard I make a conscious effort to normalize errors in the writing process through a wise intervention called direct labeling. Direct labeling is where a teacher directly and carefully labels an activity at the exact moment where a student's definition of that activity is created or perpetuated (Walton & Wilson, 2018). The goal is not about eliminating *all* negative feelings that come from an experience, but instead eliminating the distress that can come from those negative feelings. For example, in the case of mistakes in writing, the goal would not be to convince students that mistakes aren't embarrassing; instead, it would be to get them to see that making mistakes doesn't make them a bad writer.

One way to directly label failure in writing as normal and even positive is to draw attention to the myriad successful published authors who have been quoted celebrating false starts and wrong turns. My favorite of these is this quote from Neil Gaiman; It's displayed prominently at the front of my classroom:

I hope that in this year to come, you make mistakes. Because if you are making mistakes, then you are making new things, trying new things, learning, living, pushing yourself, changing yourself, changing your world.

I bring my students' attention to this on the first day of the year. Students expect teachers to start the year by talking about the consequences that will happen when they make mistakes: how many points will be deducted for late work and how the teacher will respond to phones popping up in class. This makes it a particularly good moment to directly label some mistakes as being necessary steps toward later success. Down the line, I will talk about late work and phone misuse, but my first day is all about making the case that mistakes—especially when it comes to writing—are a part of what we do as writers and people when we create and push ourselves.

Of course, I don't expect direct labeling to instantly shift how my students feel about mistakes. In many ways direct labeling is about planting a seed—one that will germinate and grow if that new definition proves true. This is why once mistakes are relabeled, it is still important to look for opportunities in our feedback to reinforce the idea that errors are not necessarily bad. Two of the most common ways to do this include

- Continuously discussing errors and mistakes with excitement, not judgment. I always refer to the students' biggest problem areas as their "growth areas" because that's where we find the clearest paths to move their writing forward.
- Allowing and encouraging revisions for any piece. If no piece is ever finished, mistakes grow safer, because no mistake has to define a student eternally on a transcript.

Famous Authors on Failure

- "I have rewritten–often several times–every word I have ever published. My pencils outlast their erasers." –**Vladimir Nabokov**, *Speak, Memory*, 1966
- "I don't write easily or rapidly. My first draft usually has only a few elements worth keeping. I have to find what those are and build from them and throw out what doesn't work, or what simply is not alive." –**Susan Sontag**
- "Throw up into your typewriter every morning. Clean up every noon." –**Raymond Chandler**
- "By the time I am nearing the end of a story, the first part will have been reread and altered and corrected at least one hundred and fifty times. I am suspicious of both facility and speed. Good writing is essentially rewriting. I am positive of this." –**Roald Dahl**
- **Hemingway**: I rewrote the ending of *Farewell to Arms*, the last page of it, 39 times before I was satisfied. **Interviewer**: Was there some technical problem there? What was it that had stumped you? **Hemingway**: Getting the words right. –**Ernest Hemingway**, *The Paris Review* Interview, 1956 (Temple, 2013)

FOCUS ON EMPATHY

In the documentary *Won't You Be My Neighbor?*, one long-time member of the tech crew of *Mr. Rogers' Neighborhood* muses about how the host, Fred Rogers, did everything wrong from a TV production perspective. The crewmember noted that children's television is often ceaselessly noisy, but *Mr. Rogers' Neighborhood* was filled with silence; children's television is supposed to move fast, but *Mr. Rogers' Neighborhood* moved at a nearly glacial pace; and television shows are supposed to use their vast resources to construct elaborate costumes and sets, but *Mr. Rogers' Neighborhood* used the same ratty puppets and papier-mâché set for over 30 years. Despite these seeming missteps, the show earned consistently high ratings for five decades (Neville, 2018).

The crewmember hypthesized that the reason for the show's success despite these "mistakes" was that while kids love noise and action and pageantry, what children, and all people for that matter, love even more is feeling understood and valued—or in other words empathy. Rogers understood the power of empathy and that it isn't just some touchy-feely thing that makes people feel good; it is a highly effective and vastly underrated communication tool, especially when it comes to disarming or muting human self-defensiveness.

If we want to respond to student writing with empathy, the key is to fight the common urge to get immediately into problem-solver mode. For example, let's say that a student tells me that she has writer's block. My first inclination as a teacher is likely going to be to problem-solve by

- giving a tip ("Have you tried outlining . . . ?");
- sharing a pithy quote "(Do you know what Ta-Nehisi Coates says the cure for writer's block is? Typing!"); or
- offering a path forward ("Let's start with a little first step. What themes in *Romeo and Juliet* spoke to you . . . ?").

An empathic response, on the other hand, would require getting to the bottom of the student's feelings first and seeking to understand her before galloping toward potential solutions. An empathetic response would be something like these:

- "Tell me more about why you think you are stuck . . ."
- "Is writer's block a common issue for you?"
- "You know something similar happened to me a few weeks ago. Does it feel like . . . ?"

It is worth noting that our time is limited, so this type of empathic inquiry isn't always possible. Further, to inquire about every feeling would be exhausting for us and our students. Sometimes we should jump right into problem-solving and suggesting mode, but we have to make sure it isn't our only mode. Adding empathy on occasion takes just a moment, and just a few moments of well-deployed empathy over a semester can go a remarkably long way toward keeping our students in the safe state that is a prerequisite for serious learning.

USE PRAISE JUDICIOUSLY

My elementary school began giving out gold stars for reading during my third-grade year. The concept was simple and seemingly innocuous. A little chart went up on the wall with each of our names, and once we finished a book, we would get a gold star next to our name. When I first heard the idea, I loved it instantly. I saw myself as quite the reader—I'd read every single one of the several dozen *Wizard of Oz* books and all the *Doctor Doolittles*—and 8-year-old me saw this as an opportunity to show off.

It didn't take long, though, for me to realize that although I saw myself as a reader, there were some students who read far more than me. While I got a star every few weeks, some of my classmates got them every few days.

It was around this time that a clear turning point in my reading began. While I started the year an avid reader, I ended it as the cliché of the boy who views reading as not being cool enough to warrant his serious consideration. It wouldn't be fair to pin all my waning interest in reading on the gold stars, but considering my clear memory of that board to this day, I do think it played its own role in the decline of reading in my life, especially because gold stars, stickers, and other external prizes have been shown to negatively impact the value we assign to a given activity. In fact, this reaction of a task losing value once external rewards get introduced is so common that there is a term, *motivational crowding*, for the times when extrinsic rewards crowd out and replace the intrinsic reward of doing something (Gregory & Kaufeldt, 2015). Further, these types of extrinsic rewards have also been shown to regularly tamp down creativity, increase the risk of cheating, and encourage short-term thinking (Pink, 2009).

Although we don't give out many stars or tangible prizes in later grades, we have our share of external rewards, the two biggest of which are grades and praise.

Grades tend to get the bulk of the attention as the main problematic external reward used by secondary and postsecondary schooling, but I would argue that praise can be just as dangerous for the following reasons:

- Praise makes our brains happy, which is not always a good thing. When a paper has both praise and criticism, our brain tends to focus most of its attention on the praise at the expense of the criticism. This is especially true when grades outpace student expectations because students see no reason to focus on anything but celebrating their successes (Hattie & Clarke, 2018).

- Praise can be a major contributor to students constructing "positive" fixed mindsets. Volumes have been written in recent years concerning the damage that can come from a fixed mindset concerning a negative character trait (e.g., *I am the worst writer in class* or *I'm so dumb*), but many overlook the fact that a fixed mindset concerning a positive character trait (e.g., *I am a great writer* or *I am the smartest student in class*) can be damaging as well. Students who view their abilities as writers in these positive fixed ways often don't put in as much effort as they could (*If I am strong already, why do I need to work at it?*), push back on the writing process the hardest (*My writing is good enough already without having drafts*), or go through identity crises when an external message like a paper grade or test score contradicts their internally held identity (*I thought I was a good writer, but . . .*).

- Exaggerated praise, especially for lower performing students, can make students feel worse about themselves. When we praise a student who failed a test or produced a piece of substandard writing in vague platitudes, the message that often comes through is that we are offering praise because we don't think they can do better and pity them. Carol Dweck herself has spoken on this multiple times recently, reminding us that "empty praise can exacerbate some of the very problems that growth mindset is intended to counter" (Dweck, 2007, as cited in Gross-Loh, 2016).

When I first learned of these dangers of praise, I was slightly horrified. For years I casually peppered "Nice job" or "Good work" in the margins of student papers as largely unconscious utterances meant to serve as little boosts alongside the serious work of learning. I also made a conscious effort to effusively praise students who were struggling in the hopes that my positivity would inspire them to greater heights.

I now understand though that praise is just like any other powerful tool: When used haphazardly, as I once did, it becomes a liability or even a danger. Yet when we use praise in informed and careful ways, its positive impact can be profound. Like us all, students need affirmation for the work they've done and growth they've achieved. Praise can also help them feel as though they belong as accepted and appreciated members of the classroom, and there is no harm in reveling at least a little in life's victories. When judiciously used, praise can do these things, and it can reinforce new strategies and approaches, inspire more effort, and help build relationships—but the key words here are *when judiciously used*. Here are some guidelines for how to do that:

- Praise needs to be genuine and about something genuinely exciting. Students are bloodhounds when it comes to uncovering insincerity from adults, and fake praise tends to be interpreted by students as a clear message that they have nothing of note to actually praise.

- It is important to combine praise of students' effort with praise of the thoughtful strategies they've deployed (Dweck & Carlson-Jaquez). Linking the two reinforces the idea that strategies and effort together form the key to success in writing growth and minimizes potential pitfalls like students feeling that effort praise is just a consolation prize.

- Praise should be as specific, if not more so, than criticism. Vague praise often seeds fixed mindsets because something like "Your wording is great" could easily be translated into "You are good at wording." When we are specific, and especially when we anchor our praise to specifics on the page, praise can help students build a broader sense of competence, which in turn can lead to an increase in motivation and engagement. So instead offer something like "The comparison of his singing to a car horn is clever. Great job seeking unusual wording combinations like we discussed in our poetry unit."

- Praise should be limited. Every day, my students take huge steps forward, come to insights that I'd never even contemplated, and write with a style and voice that make me envious, and in response I want to praise it all. The trouble with doing this is that receiving praise releases dopamine in the brain, and any dopamine-releasing activity can develop into a sort of addiction if we indulge it too often. In other words, when praise becomes the expected norm, students grow addicted to our praise, which can change their focus from learning to pleasing us. Students whose top goal is to please the teacher often grow less willing to take risks, take criticism more personally and harder, and can view any paper not covered in praise as a failure (Hattie & Clarke, 2018). The antidote to this is to be selective with one's praise. As a general rule, I strive to include a maximum of two to three comments of specific praise on any given paper, and I wait for the moments that truly demand it and where it has the best chance to make a major impact.

I find it best to think about praise as a glowing fire. If used well it can calm, bring warmth, and be a catalyst for all sorts of creation, but if misapplied it can produce a lot of damage. As with fire, I use praise regularly, but I use it carefully and never lose sight of what problems a misplaced spark could create.

PROMPT NEW MEANINGS

It's not just mistakes that many students fear in the writing process. They also often fear us. Take for example a student I taught a couple years ago. I knew this student had a difficult history with writing. From what I learned from my colleagues, a semester hadn't gone by where she hadn't struggled, especially regarding getting work of substance turned in on time or turned in at all. The student acknowledged this to me early in class and told me she wanted that year to be different, and for a few weeks it was. She showed up to class every day, leaned in during class discussions, and turned in quality work. But then came our first big paper. The first deadline passed with nothing from her. This deadline was followed by another and another, and each time I asked her about these, the response was always the same. *I'm working on it. It will be in soon.* And then, once deadlines had piled high enough, she stopped showing up altogether, and for several weeks, despite email to her and calls home, her seat sat empty.

I didn't know it at the time, but the student had settled into what Cybele Raver of New York University calls the bidirectional model of self-regulation (as cited in Tough, 2016). This model argues that students who have low skills or perceived low skills will act out while in a heightened state of fear to perceived threats from their teachers. This acting out will then lead to seemingly negative (from the student's eyes) responses from the teacher that increase the level of fear that the student has of the teacher. This greater fear then primes the student to repeat or escalate those behaviors the next time, which then leads to stronger (and scarier) responses from the teacher.

What makes this bidirectional model even more complicated is that often the threats students perceive from teachers aren't actually threats. When students are primed by earlier issues with teachers or authority figures, almost any response can seem threatening. With this particular student, I never showed anger or even disappointment about her paper. More than anything I felt concern, but the student later confided that my concern itself was a threat because she really liked the class and didn't want to disappoint me. For her, my growing look of worry was the main driver of her escalating avoidance.

Working with students in these bidirectional cycles can be difficult because they don't respond in any one given way. Some students will respond to fear by talking less and some will talk more, some will criticize the assignments or the class in public ways, and others will criticize themselves quietly as they flee into their phones.

For many years, I responded to these behaviors in standard ways: I got concerned, I got upset, and I administered consequences and long talks. And the hard thing from a teaching perspective is that these weren't necessarily the wrong responses. There needs to be a consequence for a student who can't get off the phone, and a student who publicly challenges a teacher needs to be responded to in a firm, resolute manner. It is also fine to express worry. But it is important to remember that to *just* respond with consequences or worry means that we are potentially playing our role of the *bi* in the bidirectional model of self-regulation just as the student scripted it in her head.

My approach now is slightly different. I hold students accountable, but I also use a wise intervention technique called *Prompting New Meanings*, which arose from one of the most often cited studies in education: the sticky note study mentioned earlier.

If you remember, the sticky note study found that students were twice as likely to revise an essay when they received a sticky note that read, "I'm giving you these comments because I have very high expectations and I know that you can reach them," when compared to those who received a neutral sticky note that read "I'm giving you these comments so that you'll have feedback on your paper." While that result is striking, what is even more amazing is that when one digs deeper, one finds that most of the gains in the high expectation group were African American students. They were *four times* more likely to revise than African American students in the control group, with the numbers of students who revised jumping from 17% in the neutral message group to 72% in the high expectation group.

Getting a 400% increase in engagement for a group of students from one boilerplate comment on one sticky note seems ludicrous, but as Paul Tough (2016), who recounts this study in his book *Helping Children Succeed*, explains, it actually makes a lot of sense. Tough argues that the study shows that in the suburban New England school in which the study took place, many African American students likely felt low expectations from the teacher, school, or those around them. Just at the moment when the students with low expectations were getting ready to defend themselves against an onslaught of criticism from the teacher concerning their essays, they instead found a vote of confidence. For many this was enough to effectively disrupt the narrative of low expectations they'd built, which in turn cleared the way for them to act in a more academically advantageous way.

I would argue that this study also shows that there is potentially no better place to engage in prompting new meanings than in our feedback to students because feedback is so often the area where those negative cycles and beliefs our students carry are created or perpetuated. It can also be planned and scheduled ahead of time, allowing us to be more consistent and strategic than we likely could be in the often chaotic environment of the classroom.

To see an example of how we can do this, let's consider the student mentioned above. When she finally returned (against her will) to class, I made sure to respond to her work with the equivalent of a broad smile that showed that she wasn't a disappointment to me. On her first assignment, a small targeted write, I told her I was impressed that she reconnected so seamlessly with the class. On the next big paper, I pointed out two specific moments where she'd used lessons from class to progress as a writer and thinker. Of course, at the same time, I pointed out areas for her to work on, because I wanted her to see my expectations for her remained high. But in all my comments, my goal was to displace the narrative she'd formed that I was disappointed and replace it with a new narrative—one of me *truly* having faith in her. And while this student did not instantly become an A student whose work always came in on time, she never stopped attending class again and ultimately put in the work to both pass and move her reading and writing forward in significant ways.

My experience is that prompting new meanings might be the single most powerful wise intervention, if used well. Here are some keys to doing it successfully:

• The new meanings must be surgically placed. The whole idea is that they target the exact moment that a belief or behavior is reinforced or perpetuated and disrupt it, in the hopes that this will open the door for a new belief or behavior to take its place. If a student doesn't see the purpose of something, you need to figure out the wellspring of that feeling and be there with a clear and compelling reason to do it. If a student is scared, you need to figure out where that fear is the most acute and be waiting with a comfort blanket.

- Indirect messaging is usually more powerful than direct messages about new meanings because we tend to trust actions more than words. This is why wise intervention pioneers Gregory Walton and Tim Wilson (2018) argue that we must "offer people new information, place people in new situations, or structure reflection exercises and then allow people to draw new conclusions on their own" (p. 624). For example, with the student who left my class for a while, I focused on showing her the areas where I wasn't disappointed in her and making sure my responses showed unwaveringly high expectations. While I may have told her at some point that I had faith in her, it was likely the ways that I showed that faith that caused the story of me not being disappointed to stick because she was allowed to put the pieces together for herself.

- Don't be too pushy. Adolescents are fiercely independent. They need to believe that this new narrative sprang from them or many will likely reject it on principle.

- The new meaning must be honest. The sticky notes worked so well because we give students criticism because we know they can do better. I was able to get my student to see my faith because I genuinely did believe she could accomplish great things.

- Prompting a new meaning isn't always a one-time thing. While sometimes we can have a sticky note moment where one moment of new meaning leads to tectonic shifts in behavior, more often we have to revisit a new belief or story multiple times until it truly sticks.

"When Will I Write Like This in the Real World?": Using Feedback to Increase Students' Perceived Value of Writing

Author Ta-Nehisi Coates in an essay in *The Atlantic* titled "Acting French" (2014) unpacks his high school experience as one filled with red ink and failure:

> There were years when I failed the majority of my classes. . . . I failed American Literature, British Literature, Humanities, and (voilà) French. The record of failure did not end until I quit college to become a writer.

My explanation for this record is unsatisfactory: I simply never saw the point of school. I loved the long process of understanding. In school, I often felt like I was doing something else. (n.p.)

He then contrasts this a couple paragraphs later with his academic life outside of class where

I read everything I could find: *A Wrinkle In Time, David Walker's Appeal, Dragons of Autumn Twilight, Seize The Time, Deadly Bugs and Killer Insects, The Web of Spider-Man.* . . . I was a boy haunted by questions: Why do the lilies close at night? Why does my father always say, "I can dig it"? And who really killed the dinosaurs? And why is my life so unlike everything I see on TV? That feeling—the not knowing, the longing for knowing, and the eventual answer—is love and youth to me. And I have always preferred libraries to classrooms because the wide open library is the ultimate venue for this theater. (n.p.)

Coates doesn't explicitly state whether his mindset or his schooling was the main problem, but the underlying mantra he expresses here—*When am I ever going to use this in the real world?*—is undoubtedly one of the most serious problems in our school system. I have heard such sentiments uttered in halls and classrooms more times than I can count and a few bold students have even said as much directly to my face.

What makes this sentiment so dangerous is that while whole shelves of books have been written on motivation in recent years, many of those who study it closest, like Chris Hulleman (2018) of The Motivate Lab at the University of Virginia, point to motivation ultimately boiling down to a simple formula called the Expectancy-Value Theory:

> Motivation = (The Value of the Goal) x (the Expectation That I Can Make It)

When students ask "When will I use this in the real world?" what they are really saying is "What value does this have?" And according to the Expectancy-Value Theory, if we don't give them a solid answer to that, the odds are they will only work hard enough to get the grade they want. This is often called the *minimax principle* (maximum grade for minimal effort) (Fisher, Frey, & Hattie, 2016), and it explains why so many of our students who see no real value engage in a variety of less than ideal behaviors. There are those students like Coates who fail or drop out because they don't see value to school as an institution; those who chronically cut corners or put in less than optimal effort because they, as a student expressed to me on the first day of school, "just want to get a C"; and those whose effort waxes and wanes depending on the assignment because they assign value to some work and assign little or none to others.

The good news when looking at these common issues through the lens of Expectancy-Value Theory is that a huge part of the answer to increasing motivation is to build up students' perceived value, and value can be taught. The bad news is that value is notoriously hard to teach and generally cannot be taught directly. Simply telling someone that something is valuable rarely works. If it did, being a teacher, parent, and coach would be a whole lot easier. Instead, to borrow a common creative writing teaching suggestion, if we want our students to see the value in our work we must strive to show, not tell.

Everything we do in the classroom can contribute to showing our students the value. Our lesson and assignment design, energy and enthusiasm when introducing a concept, and even little details like phrasing of directions and asides can all add value. But these moments of mass-marketing have their limits because, in the end, value is a personal thing, as unique as the students in front of us. This makes our one-on-one interactions with students in our feedback the ideal place to build value. Let's look more closely at some potential ways to do that.

LINK THE WORK FROM CLASS
WITH THE IMPACT STUDENTS WANT TO MAKE

As Kelly Gallagher and Penny Kittle (2018) remind us in *180 Days*, "writing is for life, not just for school" (p. 14). Even the most resistant and distant students understand that writing can be valuable in the world. The problem is that many understand it to be valuable in the way that a great many people understand working out regularly or eating well to have value, which is to say, they see its objective value, but the level of work and sacrifice involved in doing it makes it ultimately not for them.

This means, if we want students to seriously invest in their writing, we don't just need to convince students that writing is valuable. We need to convince them that it is *more* valuable than the other options available and worth the effort they will expend. This is no easy proposition—especially because those other options include hanging out with friends, participating in chosen extracurriculars, and watching Netflix. But we do have a secret weapon: the goals the students already bring. David Yeager, professor at the University of Texas, argues that one of the most important things we can do as writing teachers is to connect the learning in our class to the impact students want to make on the world (Homayoun, 2018).

Remember the letters my students write me at the end of the each quarter (mentioned in Chapter 3)? I also do one of those assignments at the start of the year called the *Introductory Letter* (see Figure 4.1). The main goal of this letter is to learn who my students are and what they value. I've found the open-ended questions on it to be like a siren song for students. Even the most guarded students tend to gush about their hopes and dreams, how they view the world, and what really matters to them when given a blank page to do so. These gushes are gold when it comes to creating value, which is why I keep and store these letters in a folder that occupies a prominent spot in my desk.

YOUR STORY

Our first assignment for the year is for you to write me a letter that tells me your story. Specifically, in this letter I would love to learn more about these topics:

- **Tell me about you as a person**. What are you interested in? What would you like people to say about you? What are your greatest accomplishments? What aspirations and dreams do you have? What sort of impact would you like to make in the world?

- **Tell me about your story as a writer.** How do you feel about writing? What are the successes, struggles, twists, and turns you've had? What do you like to write? What do you not like to write? What are your strengths? What are areas where you want to grow? What are your writing goals this year?

- **Tell me your story as a reader.** How often do you read? What do you like to read? What books have you read most recently? What do you not like to read? What are your strengths and areas where you want to grow as a reader?

You do not need to answer every question above and can organize the letter any way that you want. The goal of this letter is to tell me about you, so feel free to add anything else that feels important and cut anything that doesn't.

FIGURE 4.1 • Introductory Letter

Once we know what matters to our students, we can begin to add brief personalized asides and lessons in verbal and written feedback that connect the content of class with their larger life goals and pursuits. These little bridges rarely take more than a few seconds, but if they form a connection between the student's goals and the work of the class, the impact on motivation and engagement can be profound. The key to building these little bridges though is not to force them, because if students feel like they are being manipulated, it could have the opposite effect.

HAVE STUDENTS SEEK VALUE

One of the hardest things about teaching is that the learning process takes place entirely in a location into which we can never venture: the mind of a student. While we should strive to make the value of our classes clear, we can never fully understand exactly what holds value and meaning for every student.

Of course, there is one person who does have a clearer picture of what each student values—namely, the student. If we want students to view something as valuable, one of the most important things we can do is to get them seeking its value as well. Near the beginning of the chapter, I referenced a study in which researchers split up ninth graders into two groups. One group wrote a one-to-two-paragraph letter each month about how the topics in their science class were relevant to their lives, and the other group wrote a one-to-two-paragraph summary of what they'd learned over the last month. The result of that study—that the students who wrote about the relevance of the material scored nearly a grade higher than the summary group—is dramatic and points to something very important. Even brief moments where we prompt students to seek value and connection in our classes can result in dramatically more buy-in and effort.

The connection that this has to feedback is that the best way to build this student search for relevance into our classes might very well be embedding it into the reflections students do after papers and the feedback that students give to the teacher after a unit ends. Early in my career, I would often ask students at the end of a unit or big assignment questions like "What worked for you?" and "What could have been better?" These were important questions to ask, because teachers benefit when they receive feedback, too, but I now ask a few slightly different questions, including the following:

- What was useful for you from the unit?
- What changed your thinking and might help you in the future?

These questions seek the same useful feedback, but the phrasing also gets students reflecting on the value of the unit for them in the same way that the study of science classes got students thinking about the value of the class. Further, because this value-seeking is embedded in real feedback for the teacher, students often give it even more attention and weight because it has an authentic purpose and will be read closely by a truly interested audience.

BUILD VALUE THROUGH CREDIBILITY

In my experience, value is something that often follows the transitive property: "If $a = b$ and $b = c$, then $a = c$." When students find a teacher to be worthwhile and credible, the material that the teacher is teaching gains value.

As the main place where we interact with students, our feedback is a powerful place for teachers to build worth and credibility in the eyes of the students. Here are some ways to do that:

- Engage in careful listening. Credibility and care are closely linked (Stuart, 2018). When we feel someone really cares about us, we assign him more credibility, and few behaviors make us feel more cared about than someone who truly listens to us. We can do this through asking questions, noting and responding directly to interesting student ideas, and referring in the margins of papers to things the student has said in class.

- Get excited about student work. In an article in *The Atlantic* titled "How to Make Students Care About Writing" (Rizga, 2018), a 33-year-old named Pablo Rodriguez reflects on an influential writing teacher he had in high school named Pirette McKamey. One of Rodriguez's recollections was that although he was largely a C or D student before her, "she saw my strengths and it made me feel motivated. I wanted to write essays that would make Ms. McKamey love it more than anything she's ever read, and I started spending hours at the library rewriting my papers." What Rodriguez points out here is that one of McKamey's superpowers was that she got excited about student work, which, while it takes little more than a few seconds, can turn around the entire life of students like Rodriguez!

- Be consistent. Anticipatory anxiety is the fear or worry people regularly get before an activity or event, and it generally stems from unsure conditions (Gregory & Kaufeldt, 2015). I would argue anticipatory anxiety happens more often around writing because unlike many math, science, or even reading questions, writing has few concrete answers. While we can't change the subjective nature of writing, we can ensure that our responses to it are clear and consistent, allowing for some amount of certainty. Key areas we can do this in include our style of response, timing of response, and the terminology we use. Consistency in these areas, along with consistency in our voice and approach, can go a long way toward both calming students and making us appear more competent and credible.

To see this listening, excitement, and consistency at work, Figure 4.2 shows a few of my comments from an essay that a student wrote on how Emily Dickinson's innovations have influenced music. In them, I am responding in an excited way to his ideas. I'm asking occasional questions like I would in conversation. The specificity of these questions also shows that I care enough about him to know that he is an accomplished star of our school's jazz band who brings a deep understanding of musical theory. And even when offering criticism, my tone and carefully cultivated voice as an excited listener remain consistent.

It is important to mention too that my level of excitement, tone, and voice in this aren't the same as they would be in other papers. Instead, keeping in mind my role as an Interested Reader from Chapter 2, they are carefully tuned to the student and the situation. This paper was a huge leap for this particular student, so while I am still mindful of the amount of praise, the responses have the effervescent tone of someone leaning in during a conversation that I hoped would reinforce the jump in effort and depth that the student showed.

"I'm Not a Writer": Using Feedback to Help Students Identify as Writers

A large number of students enter my classroom each year with firmly entrenched identities that stand in direct opposition to what I will be teaching. Some are coy about them, but others will tell me on the first day, "I don't read" or "I am not a writer." Before a minute of the new school year has elapsed, these students have declared they will lose. Outside of the classroom they may have many skills and successes, but within the walls of my class they have already submitted to an identity of failure and mediocrity.

These fraught, nonwriterly identities that so many students walk into our rooms with matter because, as habits expert James Clear (2018) writes in *Atomic Habits*, "Your behaviors are usually a reflection of your identity. What you do is an

just like some saying a word the way they want. In the excerpt above, Dickinson capitalizes words she wants emphasized. Musicians use inflections on notes as articulations. Articulations can be used to show the peaks of a phrases and add colors to the music. But as powerful as articulations are, it is even more important to place them properly. Adding an articulation on a

slant rhyme. Slant rhymes are the perfect substitute in writing and lyrics when there is good word to rhyme. Many of today's hip-hop and rap lyrics contain slant rhymes. Rappers want to keep the flow in the song continuing no matter what. Slant rhymes can hold the phrase of the lyrics better than a forced in rhyme. In Meek Mill's hit song, *Dreams and Nightmares*, the beat come in at about halfway through the song and his first lyrics on the beat are:

dashes to show where she wants emphasized pauses. The beginnings and ends of phrases help the reader to process and understand what is being said. The pauses are just like breath marks for music. Phrasing is applied in the same way. A constant stream of words is just as difficult to understand as a musician who doesn't stop playing notes. Neither are enjoyable and make a lot of sense. The best music values the space between the notes just as much as the notes themselves. Without the concept of phrasing to guide them music would have little structure. Emily

word or scooping a note is special. But not all notes and words should have that. That lessens the impact of each special articulation. Dickinson chooses to use articulation in that phrase to emphasize tangible items. That was her stylistic choice. Musicians have to power to do the same with articulation. Joshua Redman, a jazz tenor saxophonist, has a recording of *Jig - a - Jug* where he decided to scoop only a certain note when it is played in the melody. That scoop allows him to create a pull of some sort on the note. He follows right away with a very short note after.

Comments:

Matthew John... 1:27 PM May 1 Resolve
Yes! This is a really important observation that I talk about in larger units on Dickinson, and the musical perspective on it is fascinating!

Matthew John... 1:29 PM May 1 Resolve
From a musical perspective do you have any other thoughts for why slant rhymes are so appealing?

Matthew John... 1:27 PM May 1 Resolve
Fascinating! Do you know if music was doing this at the time or does it seem like maybe she was an originator of it?

Matthew John... 1:28 PM May 1 Resolve
The example from Redman clearly shows the power of using these tools sparingly. Can you find an example from Dickinson too that shows this to take it to the next level? Tying it back to the original text will take your argument to the next level.

FIGURE 4.2 • Consistency Through Commenting

indication of the type of person you believe that you are—either consciously or nonconsciously" (p. 34). This is similar to what Carol Dweck (2007) writes in *Mindsets*, Angela Duckworth (2016) writes in *Grit*, and Brene Brown (2012) says in *Daring Greatly*: The story we tell about ourselves regarding our strengths, our weaknesses, the content of our character, and who we are or aren't lies at the geographic center of how we behave.

When students view themselves as nonwriters, they tend to behave the way they think nonwriters are supposed to behave. This means not engaging in

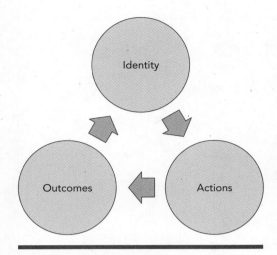

FIGURE 4.3 •

My adaptation of the Identity-Actions-Outcomes Cycle from James Clear (2018) and Dave Stuart Jr. (2018).

a writing process, not fighting through writer's block, not spending time thinking through word choice or tone, and not looking to learn writing for any other reason but to get the grade they want. The result? The outcomes that a nonwriter should expect—low scores, unengaging pieces, and lots of errors, which then reinforces the nonwriter identity and the process starts over, trapping the student in a vicious and often escalating cycle of nonwriter-ness. In image Figure 4.3 you'll see what self-identity means for our young writers:

Because of the role that identity plays in our actions and outcomes, Clear (2018) argues that "true behavior change is identity change" (p. 34). This is why getting my students to identify as writers is the North Star I point my feedback toward. I now know that this goal will not be easy; the stories we hold about ourselves don't go easily, and often it takes a whole pile of evidence to the contrary before we will even think about shifting them.

While there is no one way to help students begin to identify as writers, there are a handful of wise interventions and best practices that we can build into our feedback that can have a profound impact. Let's look more closely at what works.

FIND REAL STRENGTHS AND POINT OUT REAL VICTORIES

I have long held the notion that I was born intensely unmusical. The only class I ever got an unsatisfactory in was music in fifth grade; my friends still love to share the unfortunate story of the one time I did karaoke (seriously, don't ask); and even in my daddy-daughter music class, I have noticed my ability to keep up with the rhythmic hand gestures to be inferior to a few of the more musically attuned toddlers. While I know all about growth mindsets and am a regular evangelist for them in my classes, if I'm being honest, that understanding has still not dislodged the internal story I tell about myself about how I am "just not musical."

The problem is that while I objectively know that my fixed not-musical identity is my own construction, the history and evidence argue so clearly for it. In

Embarrassment, Tom Newkirk (2017) writes, "Self-esteem cannot be built upon the wind or empty assurances—it requires objective and publicly acknowledged demonstrations of competence; being good at something" (p. 45). Or put simply, we must see some real strengths and have real wins to point to before a negative, deficiency-based mindset can truly be dislodged.

This principle holds as true for our students who have built up firm identities as nonwriters as it does for me with music. If we want to eliminate their negative writing identities, vague and generalized half-truths won't be enough to reverse identities built on years of real failure and struggle. Instead, we need to find actual evidence to the contrary and bring it to their attention. We need to keep in mind the same question that Donald Graves (2006) asked when he first looked at a piece—*What can she do well?*—and then relay what we find to students.

But identifying current student strengths is just the start. For most students it will take more than the realization that they aren't completely terrible at all parts of writing to shift to a positive writing identity. They also need to experience real victories at real writing tasks to see that their writing is moving forward in tangible ways. Only then will many have the confidence and momentum needed to leave their negative identities behind. A couple ways to do this in feedback include the following:

• We can reference specific areas of growth by comparing and contrasting their current work with their previous work. Humans are generally more attuned to mistakes than successes, so even if students achieve lots of success, they often overlook it in favor of the few conspicuous errors they've made. By pulling up a previous work during a conference (having students share a draft digitally really helps with this) or even just referencing it briefly in written feedback, we can often make the gains more apparent, showing students that they are indeed writers.

• We can use a student's own writing as mentor texts for her. For example, if a student demonstrates mostly dull word choice in a draft, instead of pointing to professional examples, we can point to one of the areas where her word choice isn't dull. This comes with a huge potential advantage: Polished mentor texts can intimidate rather than inform students because many doubt that they could ever write like that. The same cannot be said when a student looks at a sentence she created herself. She's done it once. Why can't she do it again?

TEACH THE GROUND RULES

Many students don't see themselves as writers because they don't confidently understand how writing works. Instead, writing is a frustrating black box full of invisible tricks and rules that others seem to know but they themselves cannot see. Students who feel this way can never really build identities as writers because it is really difficult to feel like you are a part of something you don't fully understand. As writing teachers, one of our key jobs is to unveil writing so that students can see what it is and how it works. There is no place better than the individual context of our responses to student writing, as each student will come with his own constellation of understandings and misunderstandings concerning writing. Some of the most important messages to make sure that students understand include the following.

Writing Is Difficult for Everyone.

In *Bird By Bird*, Anne Lamott's (1995) handbook on writing and life, Lamott explains that

> [p]eople tend to look at successful writers who are getting their books published and maybe even doing well financially and think that they sit down at their desks every morning feeling like a million dollars, feeling great about who they are and how much talent they have and what a great story they have to tell; that they take in a few deep breaths, push back their sleeves, roll their necks a few times to get all the cricks out, and dive in, typing fully formed passages as fast as a court reporter. But this is just the fantasy of the uninitiated. I know some very great writers, writers you love who write beautifully and have made a great deal of money, and not one of them sits down routinely feeling wildly enthusiastic and confident. (p. 93)

I have found that this idea that good writing just effortlessly flows out of good writers is indeed the fantasy of a number of students; they look at both professionals and their most successful classmates and assume that, unlike them, writing is just easy for those people. I seek to disrupt this notion by normalizing the difficulty of writing by talking about it with students regularly in our conferences and in the margins of their work when I see them struggling. Sometimes I will point to pithy quotes on struggle, but I most often share stories of my students' or my own authentic moments of struggle. Sometimes I will even show them the revision history of my work to further the point (e.g., this very chapter you are reading was one of the trickiest for me to work on, with my revision history showing that I revisited and rewrote over seven distinctly different drafts over 90 distinct writing sessions). Students generally don't see this sort of struggle; they just see the final draft, look at their own initial draft, and decide that there must just be some genes that writers have that they don't.

Here Are My Unspoken Teacher Expectations.

As teachers we have lots of spoken expectations. We give students guidelines, page limits, due dates, and rubrics filled with content expectations. But there are other teacher expectations that we often don't tell students about because we never think to discuss them. Richard Haswell (2006) of Texas A&M University explores these and offers a list of moments where teacher and student expectations often diverge without either side necessarily being aware of it. These include

- Teachers often prefer a more professional style with more complex constructions and a more serious tone, while students often prefer a style closer to oral speech, one that has more basic constructions and tone.

- Teachers often view writing as an act of creation, while many students see it as an already constructed maze to be run.

- Teachers view each new sentence as an endless world of rhetorical choices, while students are constantly trying to figure out which option is right or wrong.

- Teachers put more emphasis on content than vocabulary. The opposite is true for students; hence how many of them really love to use thesauruses.

- Teachers want the unusual and new, while students often believe that the obvious and familiar are actually the better choice.

- Teachers want emotional, yet professional writing, while students often mistake professional writing for bland writing.

As teachers, these unspoken expectations often weigh heavily in our assessment of a piece, yet a great many students may have no idea that these are the things we want. This is why we need to make sure that we communicate these expectations as clearly as we communicate the page limit or due date. We not only can do this both during class instruction and co-construction of rubrics (see Chapter 2), but we also need to discuss it at the individual level because these unspoken expectation gaps are not universal and depend on each student's background and previous instruction.

This Is Your Role.

Along with how writing works and what teachers expect, many students don't clearly understand their role as the writer. Many are unsure of what the writing process should look like or how to work with feedback. This is why I make sure to tell students explicitly when they get my feedback that they need to

- Question it. I know a lot about writing, but I am not the sole repository for what makes good writing, and I make *plenty* of mistakes. This is true for all stages, too. When I hand back a summative draft, I always tell students that if they don't agree, they are welcome to respectfully question and debate a grade.

- Accept my feedback as ideas and suggestions, not ultimatums. The paper is in the end their paper, and they are in control of it. It is important that they understand that I did have a certain reaction and to weigh the possible paths I give them, but the next steps are ultimately up to them.

- Tell me what they need. Telling a teacher their needs is incredibly difficult for a lot of students. This is why in nearly all interactions I encourage them to tell me what they need and have them speak first, so they are less likely to say what they think I want them to say and more likely to say what they really need.

The Last Word on Feedback for Positive Mindsets and Beliefs

If we remember back to earlier in the chapter, the Expectancy-Value Theory of Motivation boils it down to this:

Motivation = (The Value of the Goal) × (The Expectation That I Can Make It)

While this theory is specifically about motivation, I think it also does a good job of predicting how much impact our feedback will have. When students in our classes receive our feedback, they likely run through this checklist in their heads:

VALUE	EXPECTATION
☐ Is what is written in this directly connected to a current, pressing goal in my life?	☐ Can I do what is being asked of me?
☐ Would investing in this feedback be high in rewards?	☐ What are the odds of success if I do what is being asked of me?
☐ Is what is asked of me reasonable in the time-energy cost?	☐ Is it low in risk?

If even one box is unchecked, the odds are that some assignment from another class, some extracurricular, or some social engagement will check all the boxes, and students will put their energy toward that, at the expense of seriously engaging with our feedback. This will inevitably lead to lost learning for them and lost time for us because we will have to reteach the same things again and again.

This is why we must strive in our feedback to get students checking all those boxes. And the best, most time-efficient way to do that is to find those small and critical pivot-points where mindsets and beliefs are created or continued and wisely intervene in ways that disarm the negative and cultivate the positive. Because once our students no longer fear writing, see its value, and identify as writers, that feedback you provide will cease being another thing they need to hold their nose and deal with and instead become what is really is: one of the most precious gifts they will receive from their education.

CHAPTER FIVE

Democratizing Feedback
Teaching Peer Response and Self-Review

In the early years of the marathon, dramatically faster new records popped up with regularity. After American John Hayes won the first marathon gold medal in 1908 with a time of 2:55:18, it took less than a year for a Swedish runner by the name of Thure Johansson to set a new record almost 15 minutes faster. Ten years after that, the record was 10 minutes faster, sitting just above a brisk 2 hours and 32 minutes. In a few more decades the record was 10 minutes faster still, and then 10 minutes faster another decade later.

It is around this time that the parade of dramatic new records slowed; suddenly, new records, which had commonly been minutes faster, were now only seconds faster. The official record for the marathon as I write this is 2:01:39, held by Eliud Kipchoge of Kenya. His record is less than 10 minutes faster than the record set in 1967, and many in the running community believe that it is within just a couple minutes of theoretical maximum speed for humans (Joyner, 2014).

Why is it that I am starting a chapter on peer and self-review with this history of the marathon? Because some things, while they can happen faster with better practices, are still going to take some time. Running 26.2 miles with the best training and conditions possible is still going to take roughly 2 hours. That is a lot faster than John Hayes could have ever imagined, but it is still a chunk of time.

The same thing is true when you have 140, 150, or 160 student papers in need of feedback. Like those early marathoners who shattered previous world records by 5 or 10 minutes, by using the efficiency and effectiveness practices discussed in this book, we can make some dramatic strides in a relatively brief amount of time. But like marathoners, we also face certain limiting realities. Employing best practices can enable us to give more and better feedback in less time, but there exists a hard cap on how much feedback per student is possible within the context of one calendar year—that is unless we democratize the feedback in our classes.

In this chapter we examine how we can significantly increase the amount of quality feedback in our classes by teaching students to give better feedback to each other and to themselves. Further, in doing this well, we also give our students a tremendous gift: When we teach them how to read their own work and the work of others through a writing lens, we give them the ability to extend writing lessons beyond what is covered by the teacher.

Like most things involving feedback, this is not easy. Meaningful peer and self-response is not simple or intuitive for most students, but with the right modeling, mindsets, and structures, they can learn to do both remarkably well.

The Power (and Pitfalls) of Peer Response

While it wasn't always this way, peer response is now one of the cornerstones of my writing instruction. Students first do peer response a couple weeks into the school year, and they do it for every polished paper and quite a few smaller targeted and exploratory pieces as well. We do this because peer response can be a powerful tool for student learning, if executed right, for the following reasons:

> "Anytime in which students have access to one another and are allowed and encouraged to . . . create together–co-create, co-design–that's the classroom that will be more successful than the face-forward, one way street that many of us experienced."
>
> –Patricia Kohl, 2018

- Peer response dramatically increases the amount of quality feedback students get in our classes.
- Each peer paper read acts as a model text that can seed ideas in the students for their own writing, illuminate potential paths forward, and generally provide mentorship.
- Peer response can build classroom community in a way that isn't possible when the teacher is the only reputable source of information concerning writing.

- When our students respond to each other, our multilingual students who are acquiring English receive more of that essential one-on-one time with native speakers than we teachers can likely provide.

- Maybe most exciting, analyzing the work of another can significantly improve a student's own writing by increasing their metacognition and understanding of audience and writing practices (Cho & Cho, 2011).

These positives make peer response a potent teaching tool, but like many powerful tools, if misused, peer response can have equally negative effects; it can slow writing progress, decrease classroom community, and make students less confident concerning their writing. Before moving on with how to do it right, let's quickly examine where, how, and why peer response often goes wrong, because having a good understanding of that will be key to building an approach that will work right.

At the start of each year, I anonymously poll my students concerning a wide array of writing topics, ranging from peer response to grammar to essays. And every year in every class, peer response comes back as the most reviled element of the writing class by a large margin. For example, in my most recent composition class, I received these comments concerning peer response:

- "Peer response has always made me a bit uncomfortable because I have issues with sharing my writing with other people (especially other peers). I also never feel like I'm peer reviewing correctly because I don't feel qualified to do so."

- "I don't like it. . . . People can be cruel which makes me nervous. I don't want someone bullying me again, not about my writing ability."

- "It's fine I guess but it's also not my favorite thing to do. Last semester we did them in our class and I didn't really participate in it."

- "I don't really like peer response because I never really know what comments to give and so I end up giving a couple comments about sentence structure or punctuation, and I don't like having other people read my writing, so peer review is not my favorite."

- "I personally hate peer response. It gives me high anxiety. Criticisms also are not helpful that students give me. I am also bad at reviewing others. I hate being put on the spot in front of others."

Nearly three quarters of the 32 students in that class focused in on the same themes of discomfort, anxiety, confusion, and opting out. This wasn't an anomaly; year after year, most of my students say the same things about peer response, and if I am being honest, I felt exactly the same way when I was a student. Even though I generally got pretty good grades on my writing, there was something uncomfortable and intrusive about having a fellow student—and often one I didn't know well—dig into my writing with me sitting right next to them. If I had to define it, I'd say it sort of felt like having someone rummage through and critique my underwear drawer as I sat and watched.

It should also be noted that many teachers also range from agnostic to antagonistic toward peer response, and for many years I counted myself among them. As a newer teacher, I struggled to incorporate peer response well. When I ran peer response in my classes, the results were little more than uncomfortable and relatively ineffective proofreading. By my 3rd year, I had completely eliminated it from my classroom, and for years my students did no peer response at all.

What I didn't understand at the time was that peer response, without any associated teaching or structures, invites a near perfect storm of social, logistical, and emotional challenges for the students. These must be understood and mitigated before it will live up to its potential.

PEER RESPONSE IS SOCIALLY DANGEROUS

Famed sociologist Robert Park once remarked:

> It is probably no mere historical accident that the word *person*, in its first meaning, is a mask. It is rather recognition of the fact that everyone is always and everywhere, more or less consciously, playing a role. . . . It is in these roles that we know each other; it is in these roles that we know ourselves. . . . This mask is the truer self, the self we would like to be. (Newkirk, 2017)

This idea that we wear a mask to obscure some of our features likely fits for us all at some level, but I would argue that it is especially apt for adolescents and young adults, many of whom go to great lengths to construct elaborate façades to obscure and distract from their true identities.

Peer response can be one of the most threatening places for those masks that our students wear for the following reasons:

- Our masks are designed to direct others away from our flaws, but peer response shines a bright spotlight on one's deficiencies.

- Peer review gives a real, potentially judgmental audience to our mistakes. Further, it often involves working with classmates the students don't know well, which can amplify student worries because they don't have a good sense of how their peers will react to their ideas and errors.

- Students often have "Goldilocks" concerns when working with other students. They worry about coming off as not smart enough or too smart, saying too much or too little, and being too harsh or too nice.

- A great many students are highly embarrassed about their own writing. For them, it is bad enough to share it with a teacher; sharing it with a peer can be mortifying.

Peer response is a minefield of such social risks for many students. When confronted with these issues and no tools to deal with them, many students do what is often the right choice when staring down a minefield without a working mine detector: They find ways around it.

PEER RESPONSE IS COMPLICATED

I estimate that I have worked my way through somewhere north of 10,000 student papers in my career thus far. Yet to this day, nearly every paper that I encounter is a new and unique riddle, one that takes a fair amount of struggle to solve, because writing itself is really complicated. In his essay, "The Complexities of Responding to Student Writing," Richard Haswell (2006) explains that there have been four major studies that have examined what makes writing work or not work in the minds of a reader. One found 34 competencies that play a role in a paper's success, another found 28 main criteria, another found 47 distinct traits, and still another found 46 textual and 22 contextual criteria combined with 21 other factors. The fact that academics who have studied writing for years can't even agree on what makes it work underscores just how murky and complex writing is.

People are complex, too, and when two students review each other's work, they have to navigate all the human nuance and baggage as well. We layer these two complexities when we assign peer response. It's no wonder so many students feel so underqualified that they will avoid real peer response in the way that I did as a student.

STUDENTS DON'T VALUE PEER RESPONSE

Teaching feels a bit like being the Wizard of Oz. Behind the curtain we are really just normal people trying our best, but to maintain order we often project a face to our students that is full of answers, mostly infallible, and larger than life.

One of the downsides to this approach is that a great many students have been thoroughly trained by the time they walk into our classrooms that teachers hold a monopoly on useful answers. This belief can make them instantly suspicious of the responses they get from peers. This last year a student told me, "I worry about peer review because it isn't [my classmate's] job to grade my work. Maybe if they say it's good, it might still have a lot of problems." I think viewpoints like this are incredibly common, and if not dealt with, they can largely invalidate peer response before it even begins.

Teaching Effective Peer Response

It is essential that teachers approach peer response the way we would approach any other complex, risky, and important topic: with lots and lots of direct instruction, modeling, and opportunities to practice. If we want peer response to work, we can't relegate it to a once-a-quarter sideshow that is jammed into a 49-minute period. Such a setup is a recipe for useless or even harmful peer response.

Instead, we need to make peer response a steady feature of class, one that is carefully built and revisited with regularity. Here is the blueprint I follow for doing that:

1. Help students understand that their worries about peer response are valid—and they can be mitigated with the right approach.

2. Establish and reinforce the value of peer response

3. Model the peer response process.

4. Provide plenty of opportunities for students to practice peer response.

5. Build structures that will help students be successful.

VALIDATE AND DIFFUSE WORRIES

With so many potential student worries floating around about peer response, it has little hope of being even remotely productive until those worries are unpacked, aired out, and put into context. This is why I begin my discussion of peer response by asking students an open-ended question about peer response in a Google Form: *How do you feel about peer review and response? Why?*

I urge students to be thoughtful and honest when responding to this question, because a bunch of boilerplate responses that they think the teacher wants to hear won't do much good for the activity that is built around exploring one's feelings and fears. Sometimes I will even encourage their honesty by mentioning my own mixed feelings about peer response when I was a high schooler.

Their responses dump into a document that I share with students. (This is simple using Google Forms, but if not using computers, you could have students write their feelings on the board or have an assistant compile and copy them.) Before sharing responses, I do glance through each to make sure no student wrote anything out of line, but I've found I don't need to read too closely because I know the gist of what the students will write. I've done this over 50 times at this point, and every time the majority of student responses have mirrored the responses shown earlier in the chapter.

The next step is for students to get into groups of three and engage in the protocol detailed on the next page in Figure 5.1 (a downloadable copy is available on the companion website at **resources.corwin.com/flashfeedback**). The intention of this protocol is threefold: (1) Normalize and minimize fears by sharing them aloud and helping students see that these fears don't separate but unite them; (2) draw a line between the peer response we will do in my class and any negative associations they have from previous classes; (3) set a tone of honesty, openness, assuming the best intentions, and most important, one of empathy when doing peer response.

ESTABLISH VALUE

Many students feel that peer response has minimal value, and to be fair, that has likely been the case in many of the peer response sessions they've ever had. So, right after discussing the troubles with peer review, it's useful to begin the process of establishing its value. I begin this by simply asking students why all authors need editors and readers. My experience is that letting them explore and think through why we all need reviewers brings the point home far more than any lecture from me could.

Students tend to quickly start to see the value, too. Without fail in my classes, they discuss how we as writers need readers because we often miss our own errors

PEER RESPONSE PART I:
MAKING A PROCESS THAT WORKS

Please look over the list of REAL comments from this class concerning peer review and then please do the following:

1. Highlight up to three responses that you agree with.
2. Next, once everyone in the group has read the entire sheet, go around and introduce yourselves.
3. Then have each group member explain the parts he or she connected with. During this time, just let the member whose turn it is do the speaking; don't respond yet.
4. After all group members have gone, have a whole-group conversation for 2 to 3 minutes about your experiences concerning peer responses you've done in the past and your concerns about doing peer response in this class. During this time, respond to and build on the likes and dislikes of those in the group.
5. When indicated, please use your conversations to come up with a list of informal group ground rules for how to make this peer response time effective and comfortable. For example: *It should focus on the big, important details as opposed to editing for little errors.*

FIGURE 5.1 • Protocol for New Peer Responders

or misjudge the impact our words will have on the audience. They also tend to quickly get to a point where they organically acknowledge all the people beyond teachers—friends, parents, classmates, and so on—who have helped them with their writing.

Of course, there is one thing students rarely mention that I wait until the end to discuss: that while we learn about writing by getting feedback, we might actually learn more by giving it. When we critique a piece similar to ours, we can't help but get a more accurate understanding of the task, the experience of the reader, and what makes for strong or weak writing within that context (Cho & Cho, 2011). I have found this point, when piled on top of the other reasons, to be the final nudge needed when it comes to getting students to buy into the value of peer response, as even if they don't get quality responses, they will still get something that is worth the time they invest.

MODEL THE PEER RESPONSE PROCESS

Once student worries are normalized and value established, the next step is modeling. If students don't understand what peer response should look like, it will be hard for them to truly shake off the fear that so often accompanies it. Additionally, while peer response seems to be relatively intuitive, best practices concerning peer response often defy what many students and even many teachers assume it should be.

To help with this modeling, I start with an activity I call "Watch Me Comment" that starts with me giving students a section of real student writing and asking them to give it written feedback. Figure 5.2 shows the full piece that we use throughout this exercise; you can use any sample that seems appropriate for your learners.

WATCH ME COMMENT SLIDE #1

I never grew up anywhere. When people ask me where I am from, I can only help to dread the over recited monologue of complicated family history. My mom is from Katowice Poland. My dad is from Sevilla Spain. My sister was born in America. I was born in Canada. My family is a multinational and multilingual patchwork of people knit together by a network of transatlantic threads. Throughout my life I have been surrounded by a jumble of different cultures and experiences that I learned to appreciate and let shape the way I view the world around me.

What's for dinner? I can say with certainty that this very question plagued my mom throughout my childhood. Everyday I would ask, and everyday there seemed to be an entirely and sometimes surprising new answer. As a child I envied my friends at school who ate pizza all the time for dinner. I would hungrily peer into my classmate's lunch boxes packed with chips, lunchables, and other foods that seemed like incredible feasts in my plate-sized eyes. It was not until recently that I really began to appreciate my mom's cooking. Coming from such a unique multicultural family meant that the food we ate came from all over the world. My mom is an excellent chef that never fails to prepare a delicious meal for us. I never grew up eating the way my friends ate, and learning to appreciate that was the first step in my life to appreciating and embracing my background. The food was a patchwork of styles and flavours, everything from steaming Pierogi to chilled Gazpacho soup. Food is a thread connecting my family together.

FIGURE 5.2 • Our Model Text

After students have had a few minutes to read and mark notes, I put the piece under a document camera and we comment as a class. When it comes to this particular piece, written by a student years ago, the students will key in on the transitions, mechanical issues, and how some of the lines *just don't feel right*. Occasionally, they mention a few positives like voice and word choice, because this piece has a number of strengths, too, but most of the time they go right into the negatives and stay there, piling on the criticisms when they get rolling.

I then show the actual comments I gave this piece back when I was a newish teacher, and my commenting was closer to a detached, proofreading authority than an Interested Reader, and we add these to our class-corrected document as well. Figure 5.3 shows what this looks like.

It's important to show students how a piece looks when they indulge every proofreading instinct—and how it feels to receive such commentary. I want students to see how cold and overwhelming it feels, and we talk about how easy

---

WATCH ME COMMENT SLIDE #2

I never grew up anywhere (confusing). When people ask me where I am from, I can only help to dread the (confusing too) over-recited monologue of complicated family history. My mom is from Katowice, Poland. My dad is from Sevilla, Spain. My sister was born in America. I was born in Canada. My family is a multinational and multilingual patchwork of people knit together by a network of transatlantic threads. Throughout my life, I have been surrounded by a jumble of different cultures (redundant) and experiences that I learned to appreciate and let shape the way I view the world around me.

What's for dinner(transition)? ? ~ I can say with certainty that t (wordy) This very question plagued my mom throughout my childhood. Everyday I would ask, and everyday there seemed to be an entirely different and sometimes surprising new answer. As a child, I envied my friends at school who ate pizza all the time for dinner. I would hungrily peer into my classmate's lunch (You said dinner in the last and lunch in this one) boxes, packed with chips, Llunchables, and other foods that seemed like incredible feasts in my plate-sized eyes. It was not until recently that I really began to appreciate my mom's cooking. Coming from such a unique multicultural family meant that the food we ate came from all over the world.(transition) My mom is an excellent chef who that never fails to prepare a delicious meal for us.(transition) I never grew up eating the way my friends ate, and learning to appreciate that (appreciate what?) was the first step in my life to appreciating and embracing my background. The food was a patchwork of styles and flavours, everything from steaming pPierogi to chilled gGazpacho soup. Food is a thread connecting my family together.

FIGURE 5.3 • The Detached Proofreader Approach

it is to turn away from a paper that looks like this due to shame or fear, despite the fact that there is a lot of good here. I also discuss how most of these comments relate to phrasing and punctuation, which are often best reserved for the proofreading stage, and that its overwhelming focus on negatives that makes the tone of the feedback closer to a detached judge than a collaborator.

I then offer an alternative vision to this, by giving students the guidelines shown in Figure 5.4 (and available for download from the companion website at **resources.corwin.com/flashfeedback**). Good peer response shares the same criteria: It is human, specific, prioritizes key things, and trusts itself; it is not about giving right answers.

WHAT GOOD PEER RESPONSE LOOKS LIKE

1. Good Peer Response Is Human.

The best peer responders don't approach papers as a game of find the errors. They instead respond in a warm and welcoming way that lets the reader know that a human being is on the other end. Further, they put just as much emphasis on the strengths, because these are useful for the author to know and build on. Taking a human tone that looks at positives as well as negatives also matters because it opens the author up to your suggestions; if you don't do this, there is a good chance your partner will close up and disregard your feedback.

2. Good Peer Response Is Specific.

Giving vague responses to a partner (e.g., saying that a paper is "good" or "needs better flow") is often not very helpful because those statements are far too broad. The best reviews are specific and precise. They offer suggestions such as "All the sentences in your last paragraph were pretty short, which makes this feel a bit choppy. Try making at least one of them longer to give it a more polished flow."

3. Good Peer Response Prioritizes the Key Things.

Because the goal of peer response is to help your partner improve his or her writing, it is best *not* to focus on every little issue. (Editing and proofreading come later in the process once all the bigger issues are sorted out.) At this stage, the writer wants you to focus on ideas, organization, word choice, details, and structure, and it is important not to go into too many of these things. The human brain can only absorb so many new things at once, and when we try to tackle too much, we often don't hit anything at the depth needed for the writer to truly address it.

4. Good Peer Response Isn't About Giving All the Right Answers

Your job as a peer responder is not to fix a paper. It is to give the author your perspective as a reader. With that in mind, don't feel like you need to always give

(Continued)

(Continued)

answers. Often a thoughtful question about something you don't understand or just stating your experience as you read can be more powerful and useful than seeking ways to do the author's work for them. For example, if you are confused by what the writer's argument is, you don't need to try to give them one; instead you can just say, "I'm having trouble finding a single argument that ties this together. What would you say your central argument is?"

5. Good Peer Response Trusts Itself.

You might not be an English language arts teacher, but you know when words or phrases sound wrong, when the organization of a paper confuses you, and when you are interested and/or persuaded or not. Trust that your observations are valid and worthwhile; I promise they will be!

FIGURE 5.4 • The Five Keys for Quality Peer Response

I then show them two different slides that act on these suggestions—one that points out strengths (see Figure 5.5) and one that offers constructive criticism (see Figure 5.6). These illustrate specific comments that focus on key details, don't offer all the answers, and do it all in a humane tone. They also make a case for having a balance between calling out both the strengths and areas in need of strengthening, a balance that I've found to be even more essential in peer response than in the responses from us.

WATCH ME COMMENT SLIDE #3

I never grew up anywhere. When people ask me where I am from, I can only help to dread the over recited monologue of complicated family history. My mom is from Katowice Poland. My dad is from Sevilla Spain. My sister was born in America. I was born in Canada. My family is a multinational and multilingual patchwork of people knit together by a network of transatlantic threads. Throughout my life I have been surrounded by a jumble of different cultures and experiences that I learned to appreciate and let shape the way I view the world around me.

What's for dinner? I can say with certainty that this very question plagued my mom throughout my childhood. Everyday I would ask, and everyday there seemed to be an entirely and sometimes surprising new answer. As a child I envied my friends at school who ate pizza all the time for dinner. I would hungrily peer into my classmate's lunch boxes packed with chips, lunchables, and other foods that seemed like incredible feasts in my plate-sized eyes. It was not until recently that I really began

---

to appreciate my mom's cooking. Coming from such a unique multicultural family meant that the food we ate came from all over the world. My mom is an excellent chef that never fails to prepare a delicious meal for us. I never grew up eating the way my friends ate, and learning to appreciate that was the first step in my life to appreciating and embracing my background. The food was a patchwork of styles and flavours, everything from steaming Pierogi to chilled Gazpacho soup. Food is a thread connecting my family together.

Strengths: Specific Word Choice; Repeated Themes

I love your word choice. The way that you seek out interesting words and word combinations like "patchwork of people," "transatlantic threads," and "steaming pierogi and chilled gazpacho" takes this to the next level. Also, I like that you repeat themes of things being tied together, the world, and describing specific foods. In fact, you might even be able to add more of this to make it even better!

FIGURES 5.5 • The Strengths

WATCH ME COMMENT SLIDE #4

I never grew up anywhere. When people ask me where I am from, I can only help to dread the over recited monologue of complicated family history. My mom is from Katowice Poland. My dad is from Sevilla Spain. My sister was born in America. I was born in Canada. My family is a multinational and multilingual patchwork of people knit together by a network of transatlantic threads. Throughout my life I have been surrounded by a jumble of different cultures and experiences that I learned to appreciate and let shape the way I view the world around me.

What's for dinner? I can say with certainty that this very question plagued my mom throughout my childhood. Everyday I would ask, and everyday there seemed to be an entirely and sometimes surprising new answer. As a child I envied my friends at school who ate pizza all the time for dinner. I would hungrily peer into my classmate's lunch boxes packed with chips, lunchables, and other foods that seemed like incredible feasts in my plate-sized eyes. It was not until recently that I really began to appreciate my mom's cooking. Coming from such a unique multicultural family meant that the food we ate came from all over the world. My mom is an excellent chef that never fails to prepare a delicious meal for us. I never grew up eating the way my friends ate, and learning to appreciate that was the first step in my life to appreciating and embracing my background. The food was a patchwork of styles and flavors, everything from steaming Pierogi to chilled Gazpacho soup. Food is a thread connecting my family together.

Things to Work on: Unclear/choppy lines; Transitions

(Continued)

(Continued)

Regarding what to work on, there are occasionally some lines that came across to me as hard to understand or choppy. I highlighted them in green to help. The second paragraph also has a lot of sudden transitions. To fix this, I might try to reorder it. My suggestion is to start with the line, "I never grew up eating the way my friends ate . . . ," follow this with a description of how they ate, and then end with how you ate and how you learned to appreciate it eventually.

FIGURE 5.6 • The Growth Areas

PROVIDE PLENTY OF PRACTICE

Where students really learn peer response is by getting their hands dirty, practicing again and again and again. I can't think of a writing center, secondary or postsecondary, that would ever have new reviewers critique actual student writing without also grappling with practice papers in a wide range of approaches, styles, and levels of execution. The good news from our perspective is that these practice papers can simultaneously fill two important roles: They can teach students to become better responders to each other's work, and they can push students to dive deeper into the valuable mentor texts that we would share with them even if we weren't going to do peer response.

What types of papers make the best practice papers?

There are three keys to finding good practice papers:

1. Use papers where you have student approval. Even when anonymous and from previous classes (both of which I recommend), students can find out about and be hurt by the unauthorized dissection of their work in front a class.

2. To build a stable of papers, simply ask students at the end of the semester if they can bring in copies for future class modeling and response practice. I find students are happy to share. Just be sure there are no identifying details.

3. Use good or goodish model papers instead of great papers. Having all great models is what Kelly Gallagher (2006) calls "The Grecian Urn Approach" (p. 52), when we show students lots of flawless papers, or Grecian Urns, many may infer that we expect that level of perfection from them, too. That can scare and intimidate students, which we know can negatively affect their own writing and identities.

STRUCTURE FOR SUCCESS

In his poem "Mending Wall," Robert Frost seems critical of a wall that stands between his land and his neighbor's land because, since he and his neighbor have no cattle and don't grow the same crops, it is an imaginary border to keep out a problem that doesn't exist. However, he doesn't press his neighbor too hard because he understands that his neighbor needs the fence to feel comfortable, and he even muses at the end that "[G]ood fences make good neighbors."

This same principle stands true for our students when it comes to peer response. We teachers might understand that many of the students' fears are largely imaginary. For example, it is highly unlikely that a student will blame the student responder for a low grade received, but that doesn't change the fact that our students do fear such things. This is why early on in the peer response process, it is important to build in strong structures that help students feel safe as they go through the process. While there is no one best design for these fences, and they will evolve over the course of the year, the best usually share the following characteristics.

Real Listening.

Nearly all my early peer response structures are inspired by the work from the National School Reform Faculty (NSRF, n.d.) out of Bloomington, Indiana. The NSRF has created a wide array of protocols, which is a term they use for highly structured social interactions. Their protocols are designed on the premise that groups far too often don't truly hear each other because they are too busy assessing and asserting their own roles in a conversation. The protocols are designed to remove these roadblocks to communication by eliminating the guesswork in any interaction. While the protocols vary in approach and length, what they share is a careful scripting of who will be talking and what they will be talking about at any given moment. The idea is that when we don't have to jockey for position or talking points, most people grow genuinely interested in actually hearing each other.

> Most NSRF Protocols are open source and available on their website for free. They have hundreds of protocols designed for everything from building community to talking about diversity. Check out this URL for more: https://nsrfharmony.org/protocols/

My protocols for early peer response are built around this same notion that when the speaker, topic, and process at any given time are not up for debate, it can actually make things more comfortable because it frees us up to hear each other. This can be seen in Figure 5.7, which is a common early peer response protocol; you can also download this from the companion website at **resources .corwin.com/flashfeedback**.

PEER RESPONSE PART II:
ENGAGING IN A PROCESS THAT <u>WORKS</u>

We will now begin the peer review. To start, please do the following:

1. Share your paper with your partners.
2. Pick one paper to start with; the author can preface what he or she wants the partners to notice and/or look for.
3. All three people should read the entire thing without marking.
4. Once you are done, take a couple minutes and go through and compliment two strengths of the piece. Take this part seriously and be specific with the compliments; it is equally important for an author to know what works for the audience as it is for them/him/her to know what needs work.
5. After the compliments, take a couple minutes to provide two to three <u>constructive</u> suggestions for how the author can improve the piece. When doing this, remember to focus on the "big" issues (especially the ones on the rubric). What are some important things to maybe look at?
6. When finished, take 2 to 3 minutes to talk through the strengths and growth areas; during this the author should lead and can feel free to ask questions, seek solutions, and clarify meanings.
7. Once you finish with all the papers, work on improving your piece.

FIGURE 5.7 • Good Fences Make Good Responders

Notice how the topic and the speaker are never really up for discussion. This may seem restrictive, but in early peer response sessions, I've found students respond well to these guardrails because it takes some of the social pressure off their shoulders.

Structured, Yet Unbound.

As far as I know, it is my colleague and mentor Ken McGraw who coined the phrase "structured, yet unbound," and it has stuck with me since I first heard it years ago. A conversation or response that is structured, yet unbound, has a highly narrowed range of potential topics, yet the speakers or responders have autonomy to respond in whatever way they want within the confines of those topics. In the early stages of peer response, I find that keeping the conversations structured, yet unbound, can help model best practices concerning how to respond to another person's work and make the task feel less overwhelming.

The best tool I've found for this is sentence stems, which if framed well, can act as a mentor and comfort blanket for students who need them and still provide the space for even the most advanced students to say what they feel needs to be said. Figure 5.8 provides a few of my favorite stems for new peer responders, which I often put on the board during early sessions for students to use.

When you see a clear strength:

One of this paper's major strengths is _____. A good example of this from the paper is _____.

When you see an area in need of work:

One of the areas that needs potential work in the revision is _____ because _____. A way to improve this is _____.

When you see something you like:

I liked when you said _____ because _____.

When you are confused:

Can you tell me more about _____?

FIGURE 5.8 • Sentence Stems for New Peer Responders

Gradual Release.

As students get more and more accustomed to peer response, the need for protocols and stems will grow less and less until students reach a tipping point where the protocols and stems can start to restrict thinking more than they facilitate it. That is why it's important to fade out these structures over time. There is no set timeline for doing this—it depends on the class dynamics and the students—but I do go through the same stages: Move from protocols and heavy stem usage, to protocols with more open-ended responses, to more organic collaboration with a blend of stems and open-ended responses, to true organic peer response without protocols or stems.

What do I do when students don't have a draft or won't peer respond?

The biggest logistical issue when it comes to whole-class peer response is what to do with students who don't have drafts or won't share their drafts. My answer to this is simple: Peer response is a nonnegotiable element of the class. If students miss it because they are out of class or not ready, they still must do it either during later drafting time or outside of class. These students then continue to work on drafting their pieces while the rest of the class does peer response.

Occasionally, I also come across students who refuse to engage in peer response because they are highly fearful of showing their work to others. With these students, I strive to take an empathetic approach, because forcing them will only deepen their aversions. I strive to hear them out on their concerns, and I will often offer to have early rounds of peer response done with partners of their choice, friends from outside the classroom, parents, or even me or another teacher. I then keep talking to them and keep nudging, and I haven't had a student yet who didn't eventually get to a point where he or she was willing to give it a try. Once we get there, I make sure to set the student up with a partner who will also be empathetic and offer useful feedback, because having a safe and meaningful session is often the last obstacle to these students feeling comfortable enough to regularly engage in the peer response the class does.

The Power of Self-Review

Cal State Northridge professor Kathleen Dudden Rowlands (2016) writes in an article in the *English Journal*,

> Published authors know that revision is the heart of producing effective writing. . . . Developing writers don't know this. They think of revising as a chore assigned because they aren't good writers and can't get their writing right the first time. (p. 56)

Reading this line was a revelation for me. For years, I'd struggled getting my students to do serious self-review and revision on their writing. It seemed that no matter what I did—begged, attached points, quoted famous authors extolling the importance of revision, or refused to grade a piece until it was properly revised—nothing worked to get my students to truly look at and grapple with their own writing. Instead, they often did one of two things:

1. Resisted self-review and revision and told me something along the lines of *I don't feel I need to revise/I just do one draft/I can't find any*

changes to make. These students likely came into my class viewing revision in the way that Rowlands describes, as a punishment inflicted (necessarily or unnecessarily) on them for their bad writing.

<blockquote>"Self-assessment by pupils, far from being a luxury, is in fact an essential component of formative assessment."

–Paul Black and Dylan Wiliam (1998, p. 6)</blockquote>

2. Agreed with me that self-review and revision were important and then proofread their draft for commas, apostrophes, and other minor mechanical errors before handing them back as "revised." While these students maybe agreed with Rowlands about the importance of self-review and revision, many had almost no understanding of what those things actually are or how to go about them.

Similar to peer response, getting students engaging in thoughtful self-review can have a dramatic impact on their growth as writers. In the Nation's Report Card on Writing (National Center for Education Statistics, 2011), the single biggest predictor of a student's writing score was how often he hit the backspace key, with over two thirds of students in the top quartile hitting delete over 500 times in a single timed essay. The message here is clear: Seriously looking at one's own writing and using that information to inform robust revision is the forge from which nearly all good writing springs.

Teaching Self-Review

A few years ago, the term *metacognition* suddenly appeared everywhere in education circles. Like a lot of education buzzwords, its misapplication has been sudden and rampant, with the term metacognitive slapped onto any number of products or approaches in an attempt to add legitimacy. This trend of misusing the concept hasn't been helped by the rather fuzzy definition often given for metacognition: "thinking about one's thinking." Unlike some other buzzwords, though, metacognition is one with deep academic roots, with studies pointing to its value going back more than 40 years (Brame, 2013). Further, it is a deeply useful concept because monitoring one's own thinking and processes is key to doing all sorts of things in the classroom, ranging from improving one's study habits to reading more efficiently.

The area where metacognition might have the biggest impact though is in teaching students to respond to their own writing. In a sense, the act of thinking about something one has written is thinking about one's thinking, the very definition often given to metacognition. And the good news is that metacognition can absolutely be taught. When it comes to thinking about how to teach metacognition, I prefer the way it is described in *Visible Learning for Literacy* (Palincsar, 2013, as cited in Fisher, Frey, & Hattie, 2016), which states that to grow more metacognitive we must:

1. Get to know who we are as learners

2. Understand the task ahead of us and the strategies that could be used to do the task

3. Develop the means to monitor how we are doing (pp. 92–93)

I have found that teaching self-review works best when we follow these metacognitive keys as three major steps.

TEACH STUDENTS WHO WE ALL ARE AS LEARNERS

Most students have no idea how human brains work. This is a big part of the reason they push back on self-review and revision. To help them better understand our brains and see the value of self-review and revision, I lead with a simple question: *Nearly all authors engage in extensive self-assessment and revision; why do you suppose that is true?* To make the case I might show them an early draft from a famous author, or even my own revision history for pieces I've written.

> The companion website at **resources.corwin.com/flashfeedback** has links to excellent examples of famous authors and revision online, ranging from a Ta-Nehisi Coates speech, to some images from a *Psychology Today* post titled "Crappy First Drafts of Great Books," to the famous photos snapped over Barack Obama's shoulder while he revised a speech to a Joint Session of Congress and his second inaugural address.

We then have a conversation that inevitably hits on the major reason that, in the words of Donald Murray, "[w]riting is rewriting" (Ahearn-Pierce, 2010): Our brains can only hold on to a small handful of concepts at once. Our working memory—the part of our short-term memory that we can be immediately conscious of—can hold between four to seven pieces of information (Doolittle, 2013), which is a problem when it comes to writing because writing asks us to juggle way more elements than four or even seven. For example, as we draft an essay on a piece of literature, we must think about

- The plot of the book

- Our interpretation of the book

- The audience for the piece

- Our overall structure

- Sentence structure

- Word choice

- Grammar

- Clarity

- Use of literary and rhetorical devices

- Transitions

The list goes on and on, if we let it, and no matter where it ends, it is way longer than four to seven elements.

I find that when it is made clear to students how our brains work, and consequently why self-review and revision are essential, they pretty quickly come around to the idea of doing them, setting us up for the next step, learning revision strategies.

TEACH REVISION STRATEGIES

Even once many students understand the importance of self-review, they still struggle to do it effectively. This is because the writing being reviewed in a self-review is our own, making it exceptionally hard to judge because we are too close to it.

The way to get around this block is to engage in outside protocols or strategies that prompt us to see our own work from different perspectives. While many famous writing teachers advocate using specific strategies they like or have designed, I actually prefer to teach students a wide range of strategies, because this will allow them to pick and choose the tool that is best for each situation. Some of the most effective include

- Targeted Writing Checklists: When I did the Oregon Writing Project with Linda Christensen, she shared with us that she has students do targeted revision before she will comment on their papers. To do this, she provides students with a checklist of things to look for. Some elements of her checklist remain the same on each assignment (thus training students to always look for them) and others vary in connection with the assignment. This suggestion is similar to what Georgia Heard (2014) advocates in her book *The Revision Toolbox: Teaching Techniques That Work*. Heard recommends students reread their papers multiple times with different lenses in an effort to help them "resee" their papers in different ways. Figure 5.9 provides an example of what this checklist approach for "reseeing" can look like. In our personal essay unit (where the students write a college essay, cover letter, scholarship application, or some other form of real-world personal essay), we discuss how personal essays tend to succeed when they have strong introductions, active constructions, varied sentence structure, lots of indirect characterization, and few clichés. This checklist is one that students do toward the end of their drafting; its goal is to focus the students on these essay keys one more time.

A WRITING REVIEW: YOUR PERSONAL ESSAY

Please look over your paper and check the following:

☐ **Introduction**

Look at the introduction. Our mentor introductions used stories, scenes, and surprising facts to capture the reader's interest. How does yours compare to those? Do you use similar techniques or something else? Whatever you used, explain your approach and/or technique next to the first line. Then, once you've labeled your approach and/or technique, think about whether your intro feels as strong as the models. If it doesn't, try to improve it to make it stronger.

☐ **Linking Verbs**

Do a quick count of how many conjugations of *to be* you have on your first page. If you have more than five or six, look to eliminate some. If you have fewer than five or six, think about if there are any that need to be eliminated (remember, having some is fine; it's when you have too many that *to be* begins to be a problem).

☐ **Sentence Length and Parallel Structure**

Do a look for sentence length. Do you vary it? Is it used purposefully? Is there thoughtful parallel structure?

☐ **Characterization**

Look at how you explain who you are. Make a list in your notebook of the direct things you say about yourself and the indirect things you show. In looking at that list, is there any way to indirectly show some of the things you directly say? Generally speaking, showing is stronger than telling, so try to convert as many of the direct ones into indirect ones as you can.

☐ **Clichés**

Go on a cliché hunt. Highlight all potential college essay clichés (like, "I'm passionate about helping others, which is why I want to be a doctor") and replace

---

as many as possible with personal stories and details (such as, "I have a cousin who spent the majority of his childhood in the hospital. I spent many long nights watching his doctors work . . .").

☐ **Everything Else**

After everything above, read it again (or more than once) for other key things. In doing this, think about other elements we've talked about and where you've struggled with previous papers.

FIGURE 5.9 • An Example of a Targeted Checklist

- RADaR: RADaR stands for replace, add, delete, and reorder (Anderson & Gallagher, 2012). When I use this tool with students, I find it works best to give specifics concerning the replacements, additions, deletions, and moments of reorganization, otherwise they often say they don't know what to add, delete, or change. For example, if students are writing a narrative, I might tell them to at a minimum replace the three weakest words, add two more moments of imagery, delete three lines that don't add much characterization or action, and move at least one part of the story to another part.

- Donald Graves and Penny Kittle (2005) suggest having students reread papers to find a "heartbeat line" that lies at the core of what the paper is about. I have found this to be a wonderful tool for students to use to test the clarity of both their essays and narratives, and sometimes I will even have students do it for each paragraph as well as the paper as a whole.

TEACH STUDENTS HOW TO MONITOR THEIR UNDERSTANDING

The hardest part of metacognition for many is monitoring understanding and performance. It is one thing to know who we are as learners or to remember some strategies; it is a whole other cognitive level to monitor one's self and performance in real time. Unfortunately, there are few packaged tools or acronyms to aid with this, but there are some approaches we can take that will improve students' abilities to monitor themselves over time:

- Show lots of mentor texts: Stephen King, when asked how one becomes a writer said, "If you want to be a writer, you must do two things above all others: read a lot and write a lot" (Monet, 2018). In other words, before we can have the ability to thoughtfully monitor what we've written, we need to have experienced lots of writing—good, bad, and otherwise. That base of experience forms the foundation of our ability to judge our own writing; when we look at our own prose, we can compare it with all the other prose we've seen. This is why before my students write anything in any genre, we look at a number of mentor texts—texts that teach them what works and what doesn't within the walls of that genre.

- Read with a writer's eye. In *Best Practices in Writing Instruction*, Steve Graham and Charles MacArthur (2013) suggest that students while drafting should engage in what they call reading with a writer's eye. This is where a student reads an outside published piece purely from the perspective of improving their own current piece of writing, which Graham and MacArthur claim improves metacognition. I, too, have found this approach to improve students' ability to monitor their own work, though I would add that it can be valuable to read with a writer's eye both professional and student examples that showcase effective and ineffective approaches.

- Give them time. Maybe the most important monitoring key of all is to simply give students time to revise. Linda Christensen (2009) writes in *Teaching for Joy and Justice* that she gives students 3 to 4 days of drafting time, which includes significant time for revising. I strive for the same, because I find that once students understand the power of revision and how to do it, poor revision is often more a matter of not having the time than a matter of not having the will or the way.

The Last Word on Peer Response and Self-Review

The biggest worry I often hear about the peer response and self-review processes outlined in this chapter is the amount of time that they require. This is a fair concern. Going through these steps does take some up-front time, but it is also true that much of it—regular critiquing of mentor texts, learning about the importance of a writing process, reading with a writer's eye—are all high-impact teaching moves that should probably be a part of any writing classroom. Further, the democratization of feedback opens up the opportunity to fill one's classroom with exponentially more feedback than we could ever provide alone, strengthens student understanding of their own work and our responses to it, and gives them what is maybe the greatest gift of all—the ability to continue getting and receiving quality feedback even after the bell rings on our classes for the last time. Considering all that, the payoff seems well worth the initial time invested.

Epilogue

At the start of the book I shared a question asked by Edwin Hopkins to open the very first volume of *the English Journal* in 1912—a question that has served as a white whale for a great many writing teachers in the century since:

Can good composition teaching be done under present conditions?

His answer?

No.

There are simply too many students, far too many papers, and not enough support.

One-hundred eight years later, it would be hard to argue that things are better. Further, there are myriad additional pressures and demands that writing teachers face today that their counterparts a century ago could hardly have dreamed of, ranging from email to labyrinthian teacher evaluation rubrics.

Yet even still, I have a different answer to Hopkins's question:

Yes. Good composition teaching can be done today under our present conditions.

While I would love more support and a reduction in students, papers, classes, and hoops to jump through—and I think we should keep fighting for these things—it is possible to teach writing at incredibly high levels, even when more kids than desks populate some of our classes.

The proof? Since that moment during my 3rd year when my paper load pushed me to seriously entertain leaving the classroom, my class sizes and responsibilities have only increased. But I no longer grade during lunch, oil changes, hockey games, early in the morning, or after the sun has set, and my weekends and personal days are for me, not my students' papers. At the same time, my students regularly grow in their writing skills and love of writing in ways that would have thrilled and astounded my 3rd-year self.

The key to this shift is that I have stopped subscribing to the old story that I bought into as a new teacher: The story that the inescapable lot of the writing teacher is to be constantly harried, hurried, and overwhelmed by endless stacks of papers. I have also stopped subscribing to old orthodoxies that generally come with this story about how we need to mark every thought we have, read every word students write, stay at school far too late far too often, and "correct" papers like a copy editor.

I have embraced a new story. One where practices and strategies created by innovative teachers and insightful researchers who came before enable us to be more effective and more efficient than they were. One where proficient student writers are the norm, not exceptions. One where writing can be taught well without having to sacrifice our evenings, weekends, hobbies, health, relationships, and (far too often) careers themselves. One where an impossible job becomes possible and former impossibilities like students enjoying writing essays or effectively critiquing each other's work become commonplace.

My hope is this book helps you tell a similar story because few things matter more than what you do. At the end of his 1912 article, Edwin Hopkins makes an impassioned plea for more investment in teachers of writing, pointing out that writing is so often a prerequisite to personal and professional success. On these points he is indeed right. Writing teachers change lives and deserve investment—investment that, whether states or schools sink more resources into education next year, can start today by figuring out ways to give better feedback, faster.

References

Ahearn-Pierce, S. (2010). Donald Murry remembered. Retrieved from https://www.nwp.org/cs/public/print/resource/3078

American Psychological Association. (2006). Multitasking: Switching costs. Retrieved from https://www.apa.org/research/action/multitask

Anderson, C. (2018). What is a writing conference? Retrieved from https://blog.heinemann.com/what-is-a-writing-conference

Anderson, J., & Gallagher, K. (2012). *Writing coach: Writing and grammar for the 21st century*. New York, NY: Pearson.

Applebee, R. (1966). National study of high school English programs: A record of English teaching today. *English Journal, 55*(3), 278–279.

Beck, J. (2018). Why we forget most of the books we read: And the movies and TV shows we watch. *Atlantic*. Retrieved from https://www.theatlantic.com/science/archive/2018/01/what-was-this-article-about-again/551603/

Belanger, J., & Allingham, P. V. (2004). Technical report. *Using "think aloud" methods to investigate the processes secondary school students use to respond to their teachers' comments on their written work*. Vancouver, Canada: University of British Columbia.

Bill & Melinda Gates Foundation & Scholastic. (2012). *Primary sources: 2012: America's teachers on the teaching profession*. Retrieved from http://mediaroom.scholastic.com/files/ps_fullreport.pdf

Black, P., Harrison, C., Lee, C., Marshall, B., & Wiliam, D. (2004). Working inside the black box: Assessment for learning in the classroom. *Phi Delta Kappan, 86*(1). doi:10.1177/003172170408600105

Black, P., & Wiliam, D. (1998). Inside the block box: Raising standards through classroom assessment. *Phi Delta Kappa, 80*(2), 1–13. Retrieved from https://www.rdc.udel.edu/wp-content/uploads/2015/04/InsideBlackBox.pdf

Brame, C. (2013). *Thinking about metacognition*. Nashville, TN: Vanderbilt University. Retrieved from https://cft.vanderbilt.edu/2013/01/thinking-about-metacognition/

Brown, B. (2012a). *Daring greatly: How the courage to be vulnerable transforms the way we live, love, parent, and lead*. New York, NY: Avery.

Brown, B. (2012b). Listening to shame. Retrieved from https://www.ted.com/talks/brene_brown_listening_to_shame/transcript?language=en

Buckingham, M., & Goodall, A. (2019). The feedback fallacy. *Harvard Business Review*. Retrieved from https://hbr.org/2019/03/the-feedback-fallacy

Campus Wellness. (n.d.). Curve of forgetting. *University of Waterloo*. Retrieved from https://uwaterloo.ca/campus-wellness/curve-forgetting

Chanock, K. (2000). Comments on essays: Do students understand what tutors write? *Teaching in Higher Education, 5*(1), 96–105.

Cho, Y. H., & Cho, K. (2011). Peer reviewers learn from giving comments. *Instructional Science, 39*(5), 629–643. doi:10.1007/s11251-010-9146-1

Christensen, L. (2009). *Teaching for joy and justice*. Milwaukee, WI: Rethinking Schools.

Clear, J. (2018). *Atomic habits: Tiny changes, remarkable results*. New York, NY: Avery.

Coates, T. (2014). Acting French. *Atlantic*. Retrieved from https://www.theatlantic.com/education/archive/2014/08/acting-french/375743/

Cohen, G. L., & Garcia, J. (2014). Educational theory, practice and policy and the wisdom of social psychology policy. *Insights from the Behavioral and Brain Sciences*, *1*(1), 13–20. doi:10.1177/2372732214551559

Costa, A. L., & Kallick, B. (2008). Learning through reflection. In A. L. Costa & B. Kallick (Eds.), *Learning and leaning with habits of mind: 16 essential characteristics for success* (pp. 221–235). Alexandria, VA: ASCD. Retrieved from http://www.ascd.org/publications/books/108008/chapters/Learning-Through-Reflection.aspx

Coyle, D. (2009). *The talent code: Greatness isn't born. It's grown. Here's how*. New York, NY: Bantam Books.

Crisp, B. (2007). Is it worth the effort? How feedback influences students' subsequent submission of assessable work. *Assessment and Evaluation in Higher Education*, *32*(5), 571–581. https://doi.org/10.1080/02602930601116912

Cruz, M. C., & Teachers College Reading and Writing Project, Columbia. (2015). *The unstoppable writing teacher: Real strategies for the real classroom*. Retrieved from https://www.heinemann.com/products/e06248.aspx

Desautels, L. (2018). Connections go a long way for students with trauma. *Edutopia*. Retrieved from https://www.edutopia.org/article/connections-go-long-way-students-trauma

Doolittle, P. (2013, November). *Peter Doolittle: How your "working memory" makes sense of the world* [Video file]. Retrieved from https://www.youtube.com/watch?v=UWKvpFZJwcE

Duckworth, A. (2016). *Grit: The power of passion and perseverance*. New York, NY: Scribner.

Dweck, C. (2007). *Mindset: The new psychology of success*. New York, NY: Ballantine Books.

Dwyer, C., & Dweck, C. H. (with Carlson-Jaquez, H.). (n.d.). Using praise to enhance student resilience and learning outcomes: Helping students "bounce back" in the face of difficulties. *American Psychological Association*. Retrieved from https://www.apa.org/education/k12/using-praise

Ebbinghaus, H. (1885). Memory: A contribution to experimental psychology. Retrieved from http://nwkpsych.rutgers.edu/~jose/courses/578_mem_learn/2012/readings/Ebbinghaus_1885.pdf

Farrington, C. A., Roderick, M., Allensworth, E., Nagaoka, J., Keyes, T. S., Johnson, D. W., & Beechum, N. O. (2012). *Teaching adolescents to become learners. The role of noncognitive factors in shaping school performance: A critical literature review*. Chicago, IL: University of Chicago Consortium on Chicago Research. Retrieved from https://consortium.uchicago.edu/publications/teaching-adolescents-become-learners-role-noncognitive-factors-shaping-school

Ferris, D. R. (1995). Student reactions to teacher response in multiple-draft composition classrooms. *TESOL Quarterly*, *29*(1), 33–53. Retrieved from DOI: 10.2307/3587804

Fisher, D., & Frey, N. (2018). Show & tell: A video column / Teachers as early warning detectors. *Mental Health in Schools*, *75*(4), 80–81.

Fisher, D., Frey, N., & Hattie, J. (2016). *Visible learning for literacy: Implementing the practices that work best to accelerate student learning.* Thousand Oaks, CA: Corwin.

Frey, N., & Fisher, D. (2013). A formative assessment system for writing improvement. *English Journal, 103*(1), 66–71. Retrieved from http://www.ncte.org/library/NCTEFiles/Resources/Journals/EJ/1031-sep2013/EJ1031Formative.pdf

Fuller, D. (1987). Teacher commentary that communicates: Practicing what we preach in the writing class. *Journal of Teaching Writing, 6*(2), 307–317. doi: 10.1177/1050651907300466

Gallagher, K. (2006). *Teaching adolescent writers.* Portsmouth, NH: Stenhouse.

Gallagher, K., & Kittle, P. (2018). *180 days: Two teachers and the quest to engage and empower adolescents.* Portsmouth, NH: Heinemann.

Gordon, B. (2017). *No more fake reading: Merging the classics with independent reading to create joyful, lifelong learners.* Thousand Oaks, CA: Corwin.

Graham S., & MacArthur, C. (2013). *Best practices in writing instruction.* New York, NY: Guilford Press.

Graham, S., & Perin, D. (2007). *Writing next: Effective strategies to improve writing of adolescents in middle and high schools. A report to the Carnegie Corporation of New York.* Washington, DC: Alliance for Excellent Education. Retrieved from https://www.carnegie.org/publications/writing-next-effective-strategies-to-improve-writing-of-adolescents-in-middle-and-high-schools/

Graves, D. (2006). *Sea of faces: The importance of knowing your students.* Portsmouth, NH: Heinemann.

Graves, D., & Kittle, P. (2005). *Inside writing: How to teach the details of craft.* Portsmouth, NH: Heinemann.

Gregory, G., & Kaufeldt, M. (2015). *The motivated brain: Improving student attention, engagement, and perseverance.* Alexandria, VA: ASCD.

Griffiths, S. (2015). How fast can YOU type? *Daily Mail.* Retrieved from https://www.dailymail.co.uk/sciencetech/article-3342394/How-fast-type-test-reveal-characters-words-manage-one-minute.html

Gross-Loh, C. (2016). How praise became a consolation prize. *Atlantic.* Retrieved from https://www.theatlantic.com/education/archive/2016/12/how-praise-became-a-consolation-prize/510845/

Hackman, M., & Morath, E. (2018, December 28). Teachers quit jobs at highest rate on record. *Wall Street Journal.* Retrieved from https://www.wsj.com/articles/teachers-quit-jobs-at-highest-rate-on-record-11545993052

Hamilton, D. M. (2015, December 22). Calming your brain during conflict. *Harvard Business Review.* Retrieved from https://hbr.org/2015/12/calming-your-brain-during-conflict

Harris, M. (1979). The overgraded paper: Another case of more is less. In G. Stafford (Ed.), *How to handle the paper load* (pp. 91–94). Urbana, IL: National Council of Teachers of English.

Hart-Davidson, B. (2014). *Describe – Evaluate – Success: Giving helpful feedback, with Bill Hart-Davidson* [Video file]. Retrieved from https://www.youtube.com/watch?v=KzdBRRQhYv4

Haswell, R. (2006, November 9). The complexities of responding to student writing; or, looking for shortcuts via the road of excess. *Across the Disciplines, 3.* Retrieved from https://wac.colostate.edu/docs/atd/articles/haswell2006.pdf

Hattie, J. (2012). *Self reported grades with John Hattie* [Video file]. Retrieved from https://vimeo.com/41465488

Hattie, J., & Clarke, E. (2018). *Visible learning feedback.* London, England: Routledge.

Hattie, J., & Timperley, H. (2007). The power of feedback. *Review of Educational Research, 77*(1), 81–112. Retrieved from http://www.columbia.edu/~mvp19/ETF/Feedback.pdf

Heard, G. (2014). *The revision toolbox: Teaching techniques that work.* Portsmouth, NH: Heinemann.

Hirsch, J. (2017). *The feedback fix: Dump the past, embrace the future, and lead the way to change.* Lanham, MD: Rowman & Littlefield.

Homayoun, A. (2018, August 13). How to motivate older kids without using rewards, punishment or fear. (No, really). *Washington Post.* Retrieved from https://www.washingtonpost.com/news/parenting/wp/2018/08/13/how-to-motivate-older-kids-without-using-rewards-punishment-or-fear-no-really/?noredirect=on&utm_term=.6b59a2f74274

Hopkins, E. (1912). Can good composition teaching be done under present conditions? *English Journal, 1*(1). Retrieved from http://www.ncte.org/journals/ej/issues/v1-1

Hulleman, C. (2018). I could be changing the world right now, but instead I'm solving for X. *Motivate Lab.* Retrieved from https://motivatelab.org/publications-2/2018/1/8/7htdy8ai7y5kvqjl6r2xvlys15d647

Hulleman, C., Kosovich, J. J., Barron, K. E., & Daniel, D. B. (2017). Making connections: Replicating and extending the utility value intervention in the classroom. *Journal of Educational Psychology, 109*(3). doi:10.1037/edu0000146

Jago, C. (2005). *Papers, papers, papers: An English teacher's survival guide.* Portsmouth, NH: Heinemann.

Johnson, E. (1962). Avoiding martyrdom in teaching writing: Some shortcuts. *English Journal, 51*(6), 399–402. doi:10.2307/810225

Joyner, M. (2014, October 31). The marathon world record time is inching closer to 2 hours. Here's what it will take for a human to pass that threshold. *Washington Post.* Retrieved from https://www.washingtonpost.com/posteverything/wp/2014/10/31/the-marathon-world-record-time-is-inching-closer-to-2-hours-heres-what-it-will-take-for-a-human-to-pass-that-threshold/?noredirect=on&utm_term=.69068a676f5b

Kahneman, D. (2011). *Thinking, fast and slow.* New York, NY: Macmillan.

Kang, S. (2016). Spaced repetition promotes efficient and effective learning: Policy implications for instruction. *Behavioral and Brain Sciences, 3*(1), 12–19. Retrieved from https://www.dartmouth.edu/~cogedlab/pubs/Kang(2016,PIBBS).pdf

Kirr, J. (2017). *Shift this!: How to implement gradual changes for MASSIVE impact in your classroom.* Farmington, MI: Dave Burgess Consulting.

Kohl, P. (2018). The social classroom. *Edutopia.* Retrieved from https://www.edutopia.org/video/social-classroom

Lamott, A. (1995). *Bird-by-bird: Some instructions on writing and life*. New York, NY: Anchor.

Lindblom, K. (2018). The rubric criterion that changed everything. Retrieved from https://edukention.wordpress.com/2018/01/02/the-rubric-criterion-that-changed-everything/

Marchetti, A., & O'Dell, R. (2015). *Writing with mentors: How to reach every writer in the room using current, engaging mentor-texts*. Portsmouth, NH: Heinemann.

Mascle, D. (2016, March 29). 7 strategies to improve conferences with writers [Web log post]. Retrieved from https://metawriting.deannamascle.com/7-strategies-improve-conferences-writers/

McGee, P. (2017). *Feedback that moves writers forward: How to escape correcting mode and transform student writing*. Thousand Oaks, CA: Corwin.

Mendelson, E. (2018). Use the five *R*s to avoid the forbidden fruitlessness of feedback. *ASCD Express 13*(9), Retrieved from http://www.ascd.org/ascd-express/vol13/1309-mendelson.aspx

Miller, E. (2016, December 7). Why you shouldn't multitask, according to an MIT neuroscientist. *Fortune*. Retrieved from http://fortune.com/2016/12/07/why-you-shouldnt-multitask/

Monet, M. (2018, January 8). "Read a lot and write a lot." *Medium*. Retrieved from https://medium.com/hopes-and-dreams-for-our-future/write-a-lot-and-read-a-lot-731877939e3c

Mourshed, M., Krawitz, M., & Dorn, E. (2017). *How to improve student educational outcomes: New insights from data analytics*. New York, NY: McKinsey & Company. Retrieved from https://www.mckinsey.com/industries/social-sector/our-insights/how-to-improve-student-educational-outcomes-new-insights-from-data-analytics

Murphy, C. (2018). *St. Martin's sourcebook for writing tutors*. New York, NY: Bedford Books.

National Center for Education Statistics. (2012). *The nation's report card: Writing 2011* (NCES 2012-470). Washington, DC: Institute of Education Sciences, U.S. Department of Education. Retrieved from https://nces.ed.gov/nationsreportcard/pdf/main2011/2012470.pdf

National School Reform Faculty. (n.d.). Our protocols. Retrieved from https://nsrfharmony.org/whatareprotocols/

Neville, M. (Director), Capotosto, C., & Ma, N. (Producers). (2018). *Won't you be my neighbor?* Los Angeles, CA: Tremolo Productions. Retrieved from https://tremoloproductions.com/film/338/wont-you-be-my-neighbor

Newkirk, T. (2017). *Embarrassment: And the emotional underlife of learning*. Portsmouth, NH: Heinemann.

Palincsar, A. S. (2013). Reciprocal teaching. In J. Hattie & E. Anderman (Eds.), *International guide to student achievement* (pp. 369–371). New York, NY: Routledge.

Patterson, J. (2018, October 2). 3 things I wish I'd understood sooner about conferring with student writers. *Partnership for Inquiry Learning*. Retrieved from https://partnership

forinquirylearning.org/3-things-i-wish-id-understood-sooner-about-conferring-with-student-writers/

Pink, D. (2009). *Drive: The surprising truth about what motivates us*. New York, NY: Riverhead Books.

Popomaronis, T. (2016). Science says you shouldn't work more than this number of hours a week: Working too much can be counterproductive and even hazardous to your health. You've been warned. *Inc*. Retrieved from https://www.inc.com/tom-popomaronis/science-says-you-shouldnt-work-more-than-this-number-of-hours-a-day.html

Rizga, K. (2018, August 8). How to make students care about writing. *Atlantic*. Retrieved from https://www.theatlantic.com/education/archive/2018/08/making-students-care-about-writing/567044/

Rodriguez, V. (2014). *The teaching brain: An evolutionary trait at the heart of education*. New York, NY: New Press.

Rowlands, K. D. (2016). Slay the monster! Replacing form-first pedagogy with effective writing instruction. *English Journal*, *105*(6), 52–58. Retrieved from http://www.ncte.org/library/NCTEFiles/Resources/Journals/EJ/1056-jul2016/EJ1056Slay.pdf

Ryan, R. M., Miniis, V., & Koestner, R. (1983). Relation of reward contingency and interpersonal context to intrinsic motivation: A review and test using cognitive evaluation theory. *Journal of Personality and Social Psychology*, *45*(4), 736–570. Retrieved from http://dx.doi.org/10.1037/0022-3514.45.4.736

Sackstein, S. (2015). *Hacking assessment: 10 ways to go gradeless in a traditional grades school*. South Euclid, OH: Times 10.

Skipper, Y., & Douglas, K. (2012). Is no praise good praise? Effects of positive feedback on children's and university students' responses to subsequent failures. *British Journal of Educational Psychology*, *82*(2), 327–339. Retrieved from https://www.ncbi.nlm.nih.gov/pubmed/22583094

Sommers, N. (1982). Responding to student writing. *College Composition and Communication*, *33*(2), 148–156. Retrieved from https://www.evergreen.edu/sites/default/files/writingcenter/docs/cv/Sommers_RespondingtoStudentWriting.pdf

SRI International. (2018). Promoting grit, tenacity, and perseverance: Critical factors for success in the 21st century. *SRI International*. Retrieved from https://www.sri.com/sites/default/files/publications/promoting-grit-tenacity-and-perseverance-critical-factors-success-21st-century.pdf

Stanton, A. (2012, February). *The clues to a great story* [Video file]. Retrieved from https://www.ted.com/talks/andrew_stanton_the_clues_to_a_great_story?language=en

Stuart, D., Jr. (2017, May 9). The pyramid of writing priorities [Web log post]. Retrieved from https://davestuartjr.com/pyramid-writing-priorities/

Stuart, D., Jr. (2018). *These six things: How to focus your teaching on what matters most*. Thousand Oaks, CA: Corwin.

Temple, E. (2013, January 14). "My pencils outlast their erasers": Great writers on the art of revision. *Atlantic*. Retrieved from https://www.theatlantic.com/entertainment/

archive/2013/01/my-pencils-outlast-their-erasers-great-writers-on-the-art-of-revision/267011/

Tough, P. (2016). *Helping children succeed: What works and why.* Boston, MA: Houghton Mifflin Harcourt.

Tucker, C. (2013). Google Docs: Grading tips and tricks [Web log post]. Retrieved from https://caitlintucker.com/2013/08/google-docs-grading-tips-tricks/

Volante, L., & Beckett, D. (2011). Formative assessment and the contemporary classroom: Synergies and tensions between research and practice. *Canadian Journal of Education, 34*(2), 239–255. Retrieved from https://files.eric.ed.gov/fulltext/EJ936752.pdf

Walton, G. M., & Wilson, T. D. (2018). Wise interventions: Psychological remedies for social and personal problems. *Psychological Review, 125*(5), 617–655. Retrieved from http://gregorywalton-stanford.weebly.com/uploads/4/9/4/4/49448111/waltonwilson2018.pdf

Will, M. (2018). 5 things to know about today's teaching force. *Education Week.* Retrieved from http://blogs.edweek.org/edweek/teacherbeat/2018/10/today_teaching_force_richard_ingersoll.html

Willingham, D. T. (2010a). Have technology and multitasking rewired how students learn? *American Educator, 34*(2), 23–28. Retrieved from https://eric.ed.gov/?id=EJ889151

Willingham, D. T. (2010b). *Why don't students like school? A cognitive scientist answers questions about how the mind works and what it means for the classroom.* San Francisco, CA: Jossey-Bass.

Wilson, M. (2006). *Rethinking rubrics in writing assessment.* Portsmouth, NH: Heinemann.

Zander, R. S., & Zander, B. (2000): *The art of possibility: Transforming professional and personal life.* New York, NY: Penguin Books.

Index

Because...

ALL TEACHERS ARE LEADERS

Impact your students' literacy skills tomorrow

TEACHING LITERACY IN THE VISIBLE LEARNING CLASSROOM, GRADES 6–12

With their expert lessons, video clips, and online resources, learn to design reading and writing experiences that foster deeper and more sophisticated expressions of literacy.

DISCIPLINARY LITERACY IN ACTION

ReLeah Lent and Marsha Voigt present a framework for teachers that keeps their subjects at the center and shows them how to pool strengths with colleagues in ongoing communities of professional learning around content-specific literacy.

THESE 6 THINGS

Take a deep breath and refocus on six known best practices—establish and strengthen key beliefs, then build knowledge and increase reading, writing, speaking and listening, and argumentation in every content area, every day.

THE TEACHER CLARITY PLAYBOOK, GRADES K–12

With abundant cross-curricular examples that span grade levels, planning templates for every step, key professional learning questions, and a PLC guide with video and PowerPoints, you have the most practical planner for designing and delivering highly effective instruction.

A SAGE Publishing Company

Helping educators make the greatest impact

CORWIN HAS ONE MISSION: to enhance education through intentional professional learning.

We build long-term relationships with our authors, educators, clients, and associations who partner with us to develop and continuously improve the best evidence-based practices that establish and support lifelong learning.